SOJOURN ON THE VELD

A Call to Ministry, Machines,
and Brotherhood in
South Africa's Age of Apartheid

Williams Boehms Norton

Insight Press, Inc.
Covington, Louisiana

Sojourn on the Veld
The True Story of a Call to Ministry, Machines, and Brotherhood in South Africa's Age of Apartheid

Copyright © 2022 by William Boehms Norton
www.billnortonauthor.com

All rights reserved. No part of this book may be reproduced, stored in a retrieval system, or transmitted in any form or by any means—electronic, mechanical, photocopy, recording, or otherwise—without the prior permission of the author, except for the inclusion of brief quotations in a review and as permitted by US copyright law.

This work chronicles events and conversations from the author's experiences and personal records. Names of non-public individuals have been changed to maintain anonymity, unless used with permission or the individual was deceased. Any name of a living individual is coincidental.

Unless otherwise indicated, all scripture quotations are taken from the HOLY BIBLE, NEW INTERNATIONAL VERSION ®. Copyright © 1973, 1978, 1984 by International Bible Society. Used by permission of Zondervan. All rights reserved.

Scripture quotations marked "The Message" are taken from THE MESSAGE, copyright © 1993, 1994, 1995, 1996, 2000, 2001, 2002. Used by permission of NavPress Publishing Group. Represented by Tyndale House Publishers, Inc., Carol Stream, Illinois 60188.

Scripture quotations marked "ESV" are from The ESV® Bible (The Holy Bible, English Standard Version ®), copyright © 2001 by Crossway, a publishing ministry of Good News Publishers. Used by permission. All rights reserved.

Front and back cover photos: circa 1980, near present day Mahikeng, North West Province, Republic of South Africa. Front cover photo by the author. Back cover photo courtesy of David Barfield, used with permission. Chapter 15 photo courtesy of Alan Plumley, used with permission. All other interior photos by the author.

Development editor: Betsy Thorpe, www.betsythorpe.com
Copy editor: Kathy Brown, www.kathybrowneditorial.com
Cover and interior design: Clyde Adams, www.clydeadamsbooks.com

ISBN: 978-0-914520-73-3.

Library of Congress Control Number: 2022938671

Published by Insight Press, Inc., P. O. Box 5077, Covington, Louisiana 70434, USA.
www.InsightPress.net

Dedicated to Mom,
Evelyn Ruth (Boehms) Norton,
1925-2018.

CONTENTS

Acknowledgments vii
Foreword viii
Introduction x
About This Book xii
Map of the Republic of South Africa - Circa 1978 xiv
Beginnings 1
The Beyond 3
The Call 13
The Escarpment 21
1978 25
The Messenger 27
The Team 39
The Arrival 45
The Sons 57
The Engineers 65
The Fellowship 75
The Hike 83
1979 91
The Lifeline 93
The Mosaic 99
The Birth 109
The Conspiracy 121
The Veld 131
Interlude: The Elephant Outside the Room 135
The Gift 147
The Hope 159
The Dragon 167

1980	177
The Future	179
The Gideons	189
The Puzzle	199
The Yoke	211
The Crucible	217
The Whirlwind	231
The Tears	243
Epilogue	251
Notes	254
Photos	257
About the Author	259

ACKNOWLEDGMENTS

Few writers carry a memoir project successfully to publication without wide assistance. My foremost appreciation goes to my wife, Lori, who read every page multiple times. You were both insightful reviewer and unshakeable encourager.

Many thanks go to teammates Duane and Bonnie Anderson, my South African brother-in-Christ Hugo Hendriks, and my forerunner-in-faith Bill Parr. Your encouragement after reviewing the initial draft gave me hope that the project would be worth the journey. And thank you, John Chynoweth, for your counsel and invaluable coordination with CRU and Campus Crusade for Christ - South Africa.

My deep appreciation goes to those who empowered my call. My thirteen extraordinary teammates made my time in Africa a joy, a time of growth, and something remarkable to write about. We are indeed a body and not "a bunch of parts." Gratitude goes to my two roommates, Joe and Mike, who lived with a dragon for far too much of our time together. And heartfelt thanks go to my faithful stateside support team: your contributions kept body and soul together and your prayers kept spirit and God in sync.

Finally, special appreciation must go to Frank and Barbara Barker, now enjoying paradise with Jesus. Their love of God, devotion to the cause of Christ, and selfless servanthood encouraged so many in their calling.

FOREWORD

Beginning with his arrival in Bophuthatswana, to his departure to a new and different ministry, I could not put this book down. I was fascinated by Bill's salvation experience that opened his heart for the call of God. This call led him to the Agape Ministry of Campus Crusade, now CRU.

The call to Agape meant raising support (translation: money). It is amazing that people of all Christian stripes and financial standing joined in. With gifts from five dollars to a thousand dollars, churches and individuals gave liberally to the mission of a young man who was caught off guard by such generosity. But that's the way God works. If there is a call, there is a way.

The two-year stint was a growing, maturing time. The growth took him from a stupefied bystander to a leadership ability that he never knew he had.

His descriptions of the African people of both colors are an eye-opening learning experience. The deepening of his understanding explored the dimensions of Africa's problems, and the world's.

I appreciated and identified with the emotions of God's call and the decisions that faith and fellowship demanded. *Sojourn on the Veld* provides great insight into Christian service, obedience, and spiritual growth.

—Reverend H. William Parr BA, MDiv
Southern Baptist Pastor and Home Missionary, retired

Bill Norton's *Sojourn on the Veld* is a twenty-first century apologetic and handbook for anyone responding to the Great Commission. As Bill unveils in this timely work of art, the tectonic plates of his soul were shifted when he made a decision to accept Christ as his personal Lord and Savior and begin a life of discipleship.

While not everyone is called to leave home for a work of mission far beyond one's comfort zone—Bill Norton was. In an engaging, lively, and thought-provoking way, he gives his reader insight into what the Holy Spirit of God can do both within and through the life of a follower of

Christ when she or he does not just hear Jesus's words, "Go ye into the world," but actually responds to them. Bill's faith and theology were put to the test, and put into practice, in a remarkable season of historic change in South Africa.

Those who read *Sojourn on the Veld* will finish not with the thought, "mission work is for them, not me" but "mission work may be for me as well."

—The Reverend Dr. Russell J. Levenson, Jr.
Rector of St. Martin's Episcopal Church, Houston, Texas

INTRODUCTION

Life can feel like sitting too close to a movie screen—it's too wide and too tall to connect all the images. So for all its visual impact, the storyline is obscured. This book, *Sojourn on the Veld*, contains an old story, some forty years old. Over the years, I laid down details of the most striking memories. But disconnected from each other, the memories were like that too-close movie; they lacked the power of a unifying narrative.

When I finally put all the episodes together and did my research to fill in the blanks, I was amazed at the connections in what I thought were chance incidents of daily life. In those long-ago events, the hand of God was weaving a storyline that stood out when seen in its entirety and lifted from foggy anecdotes to concrete events.

You will find that South Africa is captivating—naturally beautiful, culturally complex, and historically rich. At the time my team and I were assigned there, South Africa was a pariah among nations, but nothing could diminish the warmth of the people who were so welcoming, gracious, and outright fascinating. We found Africa to be baffling, but endearing; sometimes bland, but always beautiful. We saw hardship and pain and yet felt Africa's tenderness and heart-humbling goodness.

It is impossible to talk about South Africa of the late 1970s and not talk about race. The three years I spent on staff with Campus Crusade (now known as "CRU" in the US) were like an intense course on racial interaction. I witnessed racial rejection born of shallow relationships and conflicting values. And I saw the effects of racism institutionalized in rules and laws and enforced with cold resolve. But in contrast, I discovered that pursuing common goals with people of other races created mutual appreciation and admiration. And I found that inside we have the same traits hard-wired into our personalities, affirming we share the same Creator.

This is only one of fourteen stories that could be written. I could not write what my "siblings" on the team learned and what stirred their hearts. My hope is that my teammates see anew the meaningful work in which we were engaged and what God did through us. If nothing else, the story highlights the impact my teammates had on my life. And I hope it can provide closure for any of their regrets. It did that for mine.

One of my guides in this work was an Alabama author's autobiography: Rick Bragg's *All Over but the Shoutin'*. Rick Bragg is a master of memoir. It was Bragg's example of being transparent about his failings as well as triumphs that led me to sigh and reveal how often I blew it. I figured being real couldn't be all bad if used by a guy who holds a Pulitzer. Hopefully, transparency gives the story the reality it needs to be useful to others.

The intent of *Sojourn on the Veld* is to "make known among the nations what he has done" (Psalm 105:1). I hope you enjoy the story and see God at work as you turn the pages.

—Bill Norton
Dunnavant Valley, Alabama, May 2022

ABOUT THIS BOOK

I had boxes of material from which to construct this book; most memoir writers would be envious. Miraculously, after the many years, the written material was legible and the cassette tape recordings were playable.

I had three parallel timelines to draw from:

- Journals—These scribblings were the most honest as far as emotions and spiritual lessons but the journals skipped some key events. Some memories that I value today must have seemed unimportant at the time (a life lesson in itself).
- Correspondence (letters, postcards, and tape recordings)—I once noted in a letter to my family that the correspondence and recordings I sent home were my true journal. However, I occasionally omitted events that were noted in my journals, maybe to shield my family from problems.
- Prayer Letters—These printed letters distributed to supporters had only a small amount of unique material but were good for confirming events. The early letters tended to be a bit "rah-rah," meaning things sounded great when they weren't. Later in my term, the letters became more transparent.

Quotes from the timelines are included verbatim unless adjustments were needed for readability or confidentiality. The material is organized in a loose chronological order except in cases when the story is communicated better topically.

Place names were updated to the spelling currently in use today if the change was relatively minor. However, preserving the original name was sometimes necessary to better represent the time period. For example, Mafikeng (formerly Mafeking) was used instead of the current name of Mahikeng, and Swaziland was used instead of Eswatini (alternatively spelled eSwatini). Best attempts were used to determine correct spellings, and the author regrets any inadvertent misuse or misspellings.

The primary Bible translation used in this project, the New International Version (NIV), does not capitalize pronouns for deity. The NIV Preface states that the original languages do not use special pronouns for the Godhead. This convention was adopted herein. However, quoted material, including from journals, used the capitalization convention of the source.

Important non-English words and names are followed by a pair of parentheses enclosing a simple pronunciation aid. The syllables are meant to be read out loud in the way that seems most natural to an American (Southern accent optional). Common three- or four-letter English words are employed whenever possible. This process will produce sounds that give a general impression of the correct pronunciation.

MAP OF THE REPUBLIC OF SOUTH AFRICA - 1978

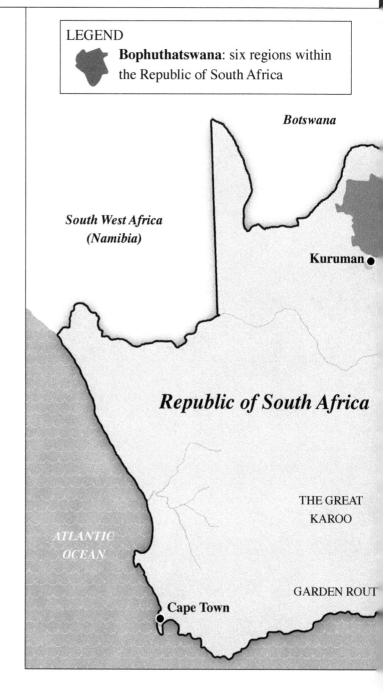

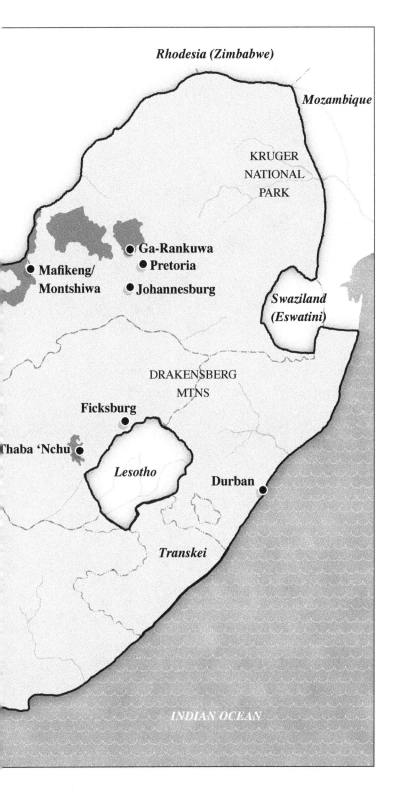

BEGINNINGS

The two most important days of your life
are the day you were born
and the day you find out why.
—Source Unknown

Chapter 1

THE BEYOND

A goat was grazing on the runway.

That was why the pilot pulled out of the landing, gunning the twin engines to gain altitude. And as the plane banked to make another approach, I could see through my passenger window that it was a rather shaggy goat, brown with white splotches. It was trotting toward a shepherd boy who was waving to us from the edge of the grass runway.

Africa wanted another pass to look us over, and for good reason. We were twenty-somethings with a peculiar assortment of skills such as home economics and road building. We originated from America's far north to its deep south, and from Delaware to the Dakotas. Africa mused: what brought these young people here, in the middle of so little?

The nine of us packed into the eight-passenger plane by filling every seat including the co-pilot's. We would join a leadership couple already at our destination, and three others arriving later, to comprise a team of fourteen missionaries. None of the team, save the leadership couple, had been to Africa before; most of us had never set foot off North America. But now, we were halfway around the world in the Republic of South Africa. It was September 1978: the apex of South Africa's apartheid era.

Earlier in the day, we had landed at the international airport in Johannesburg. We were dazed after traveling across three continents, but found our way to the gate for our puddle-jumper flight to *Mafikeng* (pronounced: ma FEE cane). Its one-room airport, manned by the browsing goat, served a tribal homeland with the exhausting name of *Bophuthatswana* (bow POO tots wa na).

In our flight to Mafikeng, we were transported to an edge of the world where Western and African cultures were locked in a forced embrace. It was an old embrace that neither would have chosen, but that neither could now escape. Our go-around landing embodied this relationship—a young boy herding livestock, as had been done for millennia, interacting with the modern aircraft. And both using the grass airstrip that was Africa's accommodation between old and new.

From my journal:

I'm in Africa. It's hard to believe but as my mind recovers from the confusion of travel it's beginning to settle in.

It is late afternoon. The sky is gray and rain clouds appear to be moving in from the west. A slight breeze lifts the pages. I sit under the branches of a thorn tree and listen to the calls of birds I have never heard before, reminding me I'm a sojourner now ...

My teammates and I were bringing our training and skills to aid the people of this land and to make known a message of hope. We loved the message so much that we put aside our homes and our futures and became sojourners so as to share it with this remote corner of Africa.

The story of how I got there starts when I discovered the message for myself.

Broken

I was a science nerd as a pre-teen, through which I learned life lessons that school omitted. For example, I narrowly avoided burning down the garage when inflating my weather balloon with hot air. Nothing in my grade school education foretold an explosion when sprinkling water on flaming gasoline. In another example, no class offered predictions for the survival of white mice in a model-rocket launch. And following an unfortunate re-entry failure, I learned science-fair judges don't value an exhibit featuring a dead mouse in a baggie. Who knew?

For a friend's birthday present, I picked out a science book on famous doctors, but my older sister, Jenny, nixed that choice as nerdy. Looked interesting to me, but Jenny said that was because I was "deep." Implying a little too deep. Maybe so deep I needed oxygen.

My other interest was a love of the outdoors that grew from family camping trips and the creeks and woods at my grandparents' farm. Even today, seeing the hills of Tennessee feels like coming home and a peek into heaven.

One of my earliest memories is my grandfather with his black leather Bible teaching the adults in the one-room Methodist Church in Shady Grove, Tennessee. My mother inherited his faith and took her children to church and revivals. When the evangelist gave an altar call, I went down front with everyone else, but only because I would have stood out if I stayed behind in the pew. The teachings of Jesus Christ were irrelevant to me. I thought science held all the answers to life I would ever need.

Siblings: Bill, Jenny, Charley, Tom, Laura

I lived through the nerd mayhem and entered the adult break-in epoch called the teenage years. I was an OK student, had wholesome friends, and went to church because my parents did. We had a large extended family in Middle Tennessee. I had roots; life was predictable. But a series of tragedies in my teenage years changed it all.

The first blow fell when my father lost his business, and my family moved to Memphis for my dad's new job. I started at a new high school.

Then, only two months after our move, my adored sister Jenny, who was a college junior, drowned while swimming alone in an indoor pool. My mom and dad were devastated.

We traveled to Nashville, our ancestral home, for the funeral. The night before, during "visitation," the funeral home was filled with grieving

SOJOURN ON THE VELD

family and friends. I ended up in the funeral home's kitchen, and comforted by one of my uncles, I wept. I wept and wept and wept. I loved my sister. She was six years older, so she had always been an adult leading the way for me and my younger siblings.

Four months after Jenny's death, while mowing an embankment in our front yard, my left foot slipped under the lawnmower. I was lying on my back in the emergency room when the doctor uncovered the injury. My mom, on my left, fainted and a nurse caught her, dropping a metal tray, which clattered across the floor. My dad, on my right, said, "Oh my God," and covered his eyes. Fortunately, flat on my back I couldn't see my mangled foot and its two missing toes.

I underwent two surgeries and spent months on crutches. For years, I couldn't hear the roar of a lawnmower engine without shivering.

Two months later, we moved to a community outside of Memphis. I assume this was for my parents to escape the memories in our Memphis house. So, I started a third high school; this time the new kid was wearing a house slipper and a limp.

The closed-packed traumas of these eight months broke the framework of life.[1] And with its loss, I sought a new "place" of my own making by rejecting the values of my upbringing. I bought into the hippie, or "freak," counterculture of the late '60s and '70s. I began playing drums with a rock band.

My family made a final move to Roanoke, Alabama. It was a life-giving change: the little town adopted our wounded family. Upon graduation from my fourth high school, my love of science led me to study engineering at a nearby university. I took my broken life framework and empty spiritual beliefs with me.

In college, I realized that the "love and peace" promoted by the "Age of Aquarius" was only a veneer. There was no universal "love," and no transcendent "peace." I found that my self-generated values provided inadequate guidance for life. I felt I was missing fulfilling experiences and relationships. I had a gnawing void from the brokenness of my teenage years.

We do not have full understanding in this life why tragedies occur.

But the void I felt inside had redemptive value because it caused me to search. I looked for completeness, meaning, raison d'etre … whatever. I searched for something to fill a hollow soul.

Searching

As I groped for answers, I found problems with my assumptions about life. I had long since adopted a god-free origin of the universe, and the theory of evolution for the origin of man.

A favorite book was the play *Inherit the Wind,* a fictionalization of the 1925 Scopes "Monkey" Trial. The defendant in the trial is accused of teaching evolution, which was illegal in the state of Tennessee at the time. The defense attorney in the play stereotypes religion and deifies science when he argues:

> In a child's power to master the multiplication table is more sanctity than in all your shouted "Amens!", "Holy, Holies!" and "Hosannahs!"[2]

However, my belief in the supremacy of science was challenged by the very laws of science that I was studying. How could a god-free universe, created by random chance, have such orderly laws? Randomness and predictability are incompatible. One of my textbooks even asserted that the engineering law stating the universe is decaying implies that a "supreme being" arranged the universe in its original, non-decayed condition.

Further, the brilliant spread of stars in the night sky of the rural South fascinated me. As I hiked the Appalachian Mountains, I marveled at the misty, forested ridges stretching to the horizon. Why did nature produce this incomparable beauty?

And last, I was confused about man. If he arose from random mutations as evolution theorized, why was consciousness produced? Why was that necessary for survival? Why did man wonder about anything beyond eating and drinking? Why did he wonder at all?

This line of reasoning kept prodding me. It whispered: There must be something Beyond nature, and something Beyond science.

In January 1974, I made these diary notes:

There is something incredibly beyond my grasp. It is the how and why of the universe. There must be a "beyond." An "all" that I cannot contemplate.

I guess my assumption that man has developed his objective mind by pure chance of evolution has holes. It has no motive. Is his ability to conceive of God necessary for his survival?

Religion simply doesn't satisfy. Why are we alive? To go to heaven? It's too cut and dried. There's something more.

Much More

In the summer of 1974, I was working in South Carolina at an industrial facility with twenty other cooperative education students, or "co-ops." Co-op students alternate semesters at school and work to graduate with experience in their major. One of my fellow co-ops, Wayne, was known as "religious."

I sought out Wayne at lunch one day because I had just read David Wilkerson's book *The Vision*. Wilkerson described a future in which America becomes more and more corrupt and how Christians should respond. For me, it brought up a new way of interpreting life: perhaps Christianity was a workable philosophy in some strange way.

As we talked across the cafeteria table, I explained to Wayne that I was rethinking my attitude toward Christianity. Wayne was not nuanced in his reply. He cut through all the metaphysical fat to the heart of my issue, saying, "Bill, you just need to be saved."

We talked about God several more times that summer. Finally, there came a day in August 1974, when sitting in Wayne's little office, I closed my eyes and prayed silently, *Jesus, if you are really there, and if you can change my life, come on in and try.*

And I meant it; I really meant it. I did not fake it as I had at the church revivals. Whatever door my heart had, I opened it for God. The prayer was so tentative that it had two conditions: *if* he was there, and *if* he could change my life. As faith goes, it was the tiniest grain of sand, but it was genuine, and being genuine, it was sufficient. The object of faith, Jesus, was much more important than the quantity of faith.

Open Heart, Blown Mind

Wayne invited me to study the Bible with him and his wife. I had heard Bible verses in church all my life, but the sounds meant nothing. But now, as Wayne explained the words of Jesus, the lens of my spiritual eyes locked onto a pivotal insight. It was like looking through a telescope or binoculars and fiddling with the focus knob when suddenly the gray blur fades into a clear, sharp picture of the moon or a distant mountain.

The insight was simply this: *I had broken the law, but Jesus took the fall.*

I had ignored the God of the universe and what he wanted me to do, and I was caught with no excuse. But Jesus Christ had accepted the punishment that I deserved so that I could go free. It was mind-blowing; why had I never heard this before?

Understanding this simple concept opened a cascade of insights.

For this truth implied a God who cared about us, and not simply cared, but deeply loved us, so much so as to die for us.

> And it implied he was the Creator, the Beyond, of all the laws of the universe, and therefore he authored the order to the universe that I was studying.
>> And if he was the Creator, then he loved the beauty in nature with which I was so enthralled.
>>> And as Creator, he was majestic himself in a way, and on a scale, that was, as I used to say about nature, *incomparable*.

And as my understanding of the Creator changed, something happened inside my heart.

I shared a windowless office with the grizzled, chain-smoking engineer I worked for that summer. His desk was in one corner, and I had a table in the opposite corner, so I had my back to him and the office door. My assignment was to review piping drawings, but I found it hard to work. This was because a feeling of elation kept welling up in my chest; it caused my eyes to water and everything to get blurry.

Behind me, the world of engineering thrashed about, but in my corner, I was surprised by an unexpected by-product of a heart opened to Jesus: *spontaneous, unbridled joy.*

Very Good

Returning to engineering classes at Auburn University, I did not know a single Jesus follower out of the thousands of students. But that deficit was corrected when I visited an open house at the Wesley Foundation, the Methodist college ministry, and through a chance but providential meeting made friends with two musicians, brothers Randy and Earl. Through their influence, I moved into the Wesley building, which was part dormitory. I was now surrounded by fellow Jesus followers: we ate meals together, we studied together, and we prayed together. I played drums with the Wesley music group that Randy and Earl had organized. We performed and spoke at churches and schools throughout the South.

On top of friends and music, a series of good things broke open my senior year. From a steady decline, my grades shot up. I was tapped to attend the national honorary convention at Notre Dame. I was invited to play with the university stage band for the summer. An opportunity came up to refurbish two houses in Roanoke; I sold one with enough profit to pay down my school loans and buy a new (used) car. This real estate project happened the same quarter that I achieved a perfect grade point while taking my heaviest course load. As my college career concluded, the engineering student council elected me the "Outstanding Auburn Engineering Graduate" for the quarter I graduated.

These accomplishments were beyond my ability before I became a Jesus follower. Jesus answered my prayer to change my life, and it was good. Very good.

Through my Wesley friends, I had made a connection with a dynamic church in Birmingham, Alabama: Briarwood Presbyterian, started by a former Navy fighter pilot named Frank Barker. Upon graduation, I took a job offer in Birmingham so I could go to Briarwood. And every Sunday the pilot-turned-pastor taught us how to follow Jesus.

In my new life as a Jesus follower, I was living out the same message of hope that I would carry to Africa. And I loved the message.

Campus Crusade for Christ, Inc. Used with permission.

Chapter 2

THE CALL

CALLING: THE MOTIVATION TO PURSUE A SPECIFIC TASK OR VOCATION ARISING FROM AN INNER SENSE OF DIVINE DIRECTION.

Ring, ring.

"Hello?"

"This is Angel Gabriel. God wants you to go to Madagascar. Tomorrow."

"What, really? This is laundry week. Who'll keep the dog? This is really not a good time."

"No excuses. Your ticket is on the refrigerator under the 'I Love My Labradoodle' magnet."

"But, but, but …"

Click.

How do you discover your calling—that's a key question, isn't it? Did I receive an angelic phone call? Nah. There were no choirs or clouds, visions or voices. However, from my experience, a calling can be discerned without angelic intervention. Seminary professor and author Howard Hendricks once said that it's hard to miss the will of God, if that's where you want to be, because God wants you there, *even more than you do*.

My calling came as I was living out the ordinary life that God had laid before me. I was working as a design engineer in my post-college job. I had fun with a great group of friends and on Sunday nights we met for fellowship in the Barkers' basement. From time to time, I'd ask out one of the young ladies in our fellowship. I led Bible studies in my apartment, and I took courses at a local seminary.

More germane to calling, I attended conferences sponsored by my church and mission agencies that encouraged potential missionaries to enlist. However, I didn't feel a desire to follow in the footsteps of missionaries after hearing stories from the mission field.

What I took away from these conferences was a sense that the words and life of Jesus were unknown in much of the world. And even where Jesus was known, little solid teaching and encouragement were available for Jesus followers. As pastor and author John Piper writes, "This is what it means to make disciples—not just that they make a profession of faith, but that they 'observe all that I have commanded you.'"[1]

These conferences also introduced me to The Agape Movement of Campus Crusade for Christ (now called "CRU" in the US). The Greek word *agape* (pronounced: uh GAH pay) is used in the Bible to describe the sacrificial love of God. The Agape ministry sent individuals with professional and vocational skills—teaching, nursing, or engineering, for example—to countries in need. These individuals would contribute to the country physically and also have a ministry to share their faith with the people of the country. The minimum commitment, after training, was two years.

I felt deeply the need for the world to know Jesus. I began to have a sense that my life, at this time of my life, could best be used in overseas ministry. I compiled this list:

> I am a committed Jesus follower.
> I am unencumbered relationally and free to travel.
> I am free from financial obligations.
> I am healthy and free from any medical issues.
> I am educated and equipped with skills that could open doors.

Investing some amount of time into missions just seemed to make sense. And Crusade's Agape ministry sounded like a good fit.

As this conclusion settled in, a world-class wrestling match developed inside of me. In one corner were the business-as-usual motivations: to continue my career and thereby help finance others to go into missions, not to mention all the things I could do for Jesus here. In the other corner were the radical motivations: the mission of Christ, the shortage of workers, and my ability to contribute.

As the wrestling raged inside, the word "go" took on a new, intense meaning. Every time I saw or heard the word "go," in any context, it caused me to brood on whether I should really do it.

One day in the summer of 1977, driving down an Alabama highway, the debate in my head got so strong that I pulled over, banged my fist on the hood of my new (used) car, and said out loud, "God, I will go wherever you want me to, even to Africa."

In this moment of zeal, it didn't occur to me that he might take me up on the offer.

But with or without zeal, I found that I could not ignore the call. I agreed with God to go into missions.

July 20, 1977 (Birmingham)

I have made one of the most important decisions of my life—to take a two-year stab at missions overseas. It means giving up a great deal I thought was important; career and future [graduate] school. It means giving up much that is important; marriage, family, home. If we can trust in God's sovereign control in our lives, he will surely not allow me to ruin my life as long as I sincerely seek his will. How then can I doubt?

It would be admirable to say that my call was due to my passion for those who didn't know about Jesus. For many missionaries that is the nature of their call, and it is a noble calling. But for me, it was more a calculated evaluation of a need and my ability to assist with this need.

To conclude: my call to missions came from not so much passion, as pondering. You mustn't forget I am an engineer.

Counselors and Critics

I began asking others for their input about this plan as directed by God's book of wisdom:

> Plans fail for lack of counsel,
> but with many advisers they succeed. (Proverbs 15:22)

For counselors, I talked to those who knew me well, who knew what the plan entailed, who were walking with God, and who would be honest and transparent. Their counsel was vital; I don't know that I would have had the confidence to do it without the encouragement of others. I did not seek out counselors who might be negative, but God provided them anyway.

My parents were supportive of my decision, though pensive. My folks had the most on the line: to carry a concern for a child is a heavy burden, especially with our family's particular past. But my father told me that, if I was going to do this, I should go now while I had the opportunity. Who knew if I would ever have the chance again?

I consulted with my pastor, Frank Barker. I sat across his desk from him, as hundreds of candidate missionaries had done, and put to him the same question that all of them asked: "Frank, what is a call to ministry; what does it look like?"

Talked with Frank. Informed him of all that had run thru my mind, what God seemed to be telling me. He said it sounded like a "call" to him.

Frank had wisdom that needed few words to nail the truth. Frank walked closely with his heavenly father; one could act on his counsel with confidence.

My friends from Briarwood and Wesley were committed to supporting missions, and many had been involved with Crusade in college. All were encouraging and even promised prayer and financial support.

However, the input from one friend had a different twist. After an explanation of the plan as I knew it at that time, he responded, "Gosh, Bill, so you are giving up your job, career, money, security, safety, friends,

marriage, family, kids, and country to be a witness for Jesus c
Wow, man, that's great."

I managed a thin smile as I thought, *Wow, man, that's a long list.*

If my friend intended to compliment my dedication, he missed the mark. I'd already thought through these sacrifices, just not all together in one run-on sentence. But this conversation was helpful, because it ensured I hadn't missed anything.

At our family reunion, the girlfriend of a relative asked me a curious question, "What if you don't like it?" I had never thought of becoming a missionary in terms of "liking it," so I shrugged off this question.

In hindsight, how should I have answered the question "what if you don't like it?" The question correctly recognizes that there is uncertainty in following a call of God. Uncertainty is risk by another name, and "liking it" is the least of the risks taken in pursuing international missions.

In this life we are always faced with uncertainty; it is a characteristic of being the created rather than the Creator. However, we can be certain of the love of the Father. It takes faith in his love to persevere in the face of uncertainty. But then, that is the essence of faith.

> Now faith is being sure of what we hope for and certain of what we do not see. (Hebrews 11:1)

I should have answered my relative's girlfriend that I didn't know if I would like it, but I trusted that God was calling me, and I knew that he loved me.

A surprising challenge came when I asked to meet with the owner of an engineering company whom I knew through business. He was wealthy and his giving back to the community was legendary. In the recesses of my mind, a thought flickered that if he knew what I was doing, maybe he would contribute to it.

When I asked to see him, his secretary said, "Sure, go on in." His office looked out over the forested hills of Birmingham and was about the size of a tennis court.

"Have a seat, Bill, what's on your mind?" the executive said.

"Thank you," I replied. "I wanted to meet with you in person to tell you about a new opportunity I am pursuing. I am planning to work for an overseas ministry where I can use my engineering. I wanted to see if you had any questions and get your feedback."

Like a good executive, my advisor cut immediately to the core decision. "In my opinion, Bill, you can serve people and the world best by staying here and working as an engineer, contributing to your church, and living a life that is an example to others."

"Well, I guess I haven't thought of it that way." I tried to dodge telling him that I had already rejected his idea. But he would not be deterred.

"That would do more good and have more impact than whatever you might do in ministry, and that is what I recommend you do," the executive continued.

"Thank you, I'll consider that." At this point, I just wanted to gracefully exit. But the executive gave no quarter. He insisted on a decision.

"So, what are you going to do now?"

"Well, I have to raise financial support ..." *Oops*.

"Thanks for coming in, Bill," interrupted the executive. And my multimillionaire acquaintance stood up in the way executives do to end a meeting.

I nodded and stumbled out of the office. It was over in minutes.

The executive's curt termination of our conversation confused and embarrassed me. In hindsight, mentioning money right after he had dismissed my plan was thickheaded.

The executive's views did not change my sense of calling. He and I had different views of the impact my life could contribute. However, the outcome of our conversation doesn't diminish my opinion of him as a good man.

The most serious challenge to my plans came from a former Crusade staff member.

August 1, 1977 (Birmingham)

Last night Janice called to play tennis. I had a feeling the Lord had a special purpose for getting us together. As a former staffer she was able to give me an inside story on the organization. A real fear and despair clouded me as we talked and she revealed her misgivings about Crusade.

I weighed Janice's views of Crusade carefully. I had to acknowledge that it was an organization full of imperfect people. Therefore, working within this organization would not be all rainbows and unicorns. Still, I concluded that for what I was called to do, it was the right vehicle.

So, my call to serve God in missions started with an intersection of need, ability, and desire and was confirmed by counsel and, later, by circumstances. All of this was overlaid with prayer. By the time all these validations ran their course, I knew my calling. A heavenly phone call would have been overkill.

However, one more confirmation was required. It's all pseudo-spiritual academics without action. Did I have the confidence in God's leading to get up and follow the call? Yes, I did.

And this was the last time I thought about my calling for the next three years, right? Nah. God's call is much more interesting than that.

Chapter 3

THE ESCARPMENT

ESCARPMENT: A SUDDEN AND BROAD ELEVATION CHANGE DUE TO A CONTINENTAL-SCALE FAULT LINE.

I've always connected the word escarpment with Johnny Weissmuller and a black-and-white Tarzan movie. The plot involved finding the ivory-laden elephant graveyard beyond some fictional escarpment. The movie reflects Africa's real-life escarpments—massive geologic features involving mountains, cliffs, and drop-offs. Life has escarpments, too, when the future can change suddenly and dramatically. Like the escarpment that loomed at the last moment in my plan to become a missionary.

I turned in my application to Campus Crusade and began the screening process in the fall of 1977. I was interviewed by two staff members based in Birmingham: a young white fellow and an older black lady who radiated spirituality—peace, acceptance, and gentleness. The interview was thorough, as it needed to be. It consisted of background and spiritual belief questions and a deep dive into why I wanted to join Campus Crusade.

After a long evaluation period, I was notified that I passed the screening: my application read well, my references were positive, and the interviewers' report was good. I was accepted to enter the new staff training program at Crusade headquarters in San Bernardino, California, in January.

Then, in late November, my precious, godly mother had a fainting spell, collapsing on her front porch in Roanoke. The ensuing medical workup revealed a congenital defect inside her heart that was explained as a "hole" between two of the chambers.[1] This was a complete surprise; she had never had any heart problems before this. Mom's doctor recommended heart surgery to apply a patch. The hospital scheduled the operation for the first opening after the holidays: January 2.

By the time the diagnosis was completed and a treatment plan was developed, I had resigned from my job and bought my plane ticket to California. I was slated to leave on January 7.

This was cutting it close. *Do I change my plan?* Mom said not to, so I didn't.

My mother's age was fifty-two and the prognosis was good, but heart surgery is, of course, inherently risky. Our circle of friends and family in Tennessee, Birmingham, Roanoke, and beyond got on their knees and prayed: *God, please heal Evelyn.*

The operation was successful. I was able to see my mother sitting up and smiling with her unquenchable grin before I boarded the flight to California. She had a smooth recovery; this particular heart problem never bothered her again.

As this crisis unfolded, I asked a question, *Why the timing, God?* This problem could have appeared at any time in my mother's life. *Why did it happen now, squarely in the middle of my radical life change?*

The arrival of this life escarpment, involving the most influential person in my life, just as I was walking out the door to ministry, was not a coincidence. God was saying, *I've got this, as I will have a path through everything else that comes up.*

In the impossible timing of this message, God provided an unmistakable confirmation of his call.

1978

Look for Christ, and you will find him,
and with him everything else.

—C. S. Lewis, *Mere Christianity*

Chapter 4

THE MESSENGER

It is tempting to say that a missionary is one who goes; after all, was not the word "go" a large part of my decision? Yes, but a missionary has a calling, and if one is called, then he or she is being sent. One who goes is simply a traveler, but one who is sent is a *messenger*.

The messengers who came to Campus Crusade to fulfill their calling received thorough preparation. Name almost any subject touching ministry or the Christian life and Crusade training was available. Crusade frequently used outside spiritual leaders to strengthen its instruction. The preparation we messengers received was second to none.

Training of Agape staff took eight months: two months in introductory staff training, two months raising financial support, then four months in international training.

New Staff Training

On January 7, 1978, I caught a red-eye flight to San Bernardino, California. The next morning, I got a ride from the airport to Campus Crusade headquarters at Arrowhead Springs, California. (The headquarters moved to Orlando, Florida, in 1980.) New staff stayed in dormitories in the training village—much like a college campus—down the hill from the headquarters.

Bag in hand, I found my room in the village. The room was lit only by the light from the door I had just opened. Out of the shadows of a lower bunk rolled this dark, barefoot figure with rumpled hair, week-old beard, mustache worthy of *Lonesome Dove,* and a torn Wyoming sweatshirt. *One of us is in the wrong place,* I thought.

The forbidding stranger held out his hand. "Hello, my name is Joe," he said. And that is how I met my lifelong friend from South Dakota. I took the top bunk over his.

Crusade kicked off training with college-level Bible and theology instruction in a mini-term called Institute for Biblical Studies (IBS). After IBS exams came the New Staff Training (NST) program, which focused on policies and ministry.

NST introduced a fundamental Crusade tool called *The Four Spiritual* Laws. This tool is a thin booklet about the size of the palm of the hand. It steps through how a person can become a Jesus follower using simple explanations and illustrations. We relied on this booklet throughout our training and field assignments.

We spent considerable time during training working through human resource requirements. Crusade's personnel administration was well organized; the Library of Congress would be put to shame at such organization. A form, checklist, or procedure had been developed for every human-resource need a staffer could encounter. For example, before leaving the country, I completed a fill-in-the-blank "Last Will and Testament" (not kidding).

Since I was tagged for international work, I had medical checkups and vaccinations. Some of the inoculations were booster shots, like smallpox and polio; some were exotic, like cholera and yellow fever.

We met several times individually with experienced Crusade staff for "check out" to ensure that we understood the material and to answer questions. I wrote home:

> *Throughout all of staff training, despite the rough schedule,*
> *I've been reassured so many times by the attention and love*
> *that new staff receive from senior staff.*

Before leaving Arrowhead Springs, we had to complete a placement request form to designate the countries where we preferred to serve. We had all day to think and pray, and then we were to leave our completed forms in a wire basket in the classroom. No promises were given on our assignment, but it was nice of them to ask.

I thought about it—not long enough—and got inspired. I was *"all fired up,"* as we say in the parlance of Alabama. I wrote across my placement form, "I want to be placed anywhere that Crusade has never served before." I dropped off the form, smug in my spirituality: I was offering to open new ground for the worldwide Crusade ministry. What faith!

Back in my bunk room, my "faith," more like bravado, wavered. I re-thought my action, *"Anywhere, Bill? Really?"* I trotted back to the classroom, but the wire basket was empty; the forms had already been gathered up. I decided to let it go; retrieving it now would validate my idiocy. I would let God take it from here.

A verse from the book of John can be applied to the location of God's calling.

> The wind blows wherever it pleases. You hear its sound, but you cannot tell where it comes from or where it is going. So it is with everyone born of the Spirit. (John 3:8)

On the plane to California, I wrote my parents about this passage of scripture:

> *As I've wrestled with the question of going into missions I've come to see a lot of the meaning in that verse [John 3:8]. I've known God is leading, and I can see the effects of it, but often I've wondered to him: Lord, where are you taking me?*

As it turned out, God fulfilled my request to open a new Crusade location in a way impossible to have foreseen. Just as surprising, I have been grateful for a lifetime that he did.

Piece o' Cake

In late February, I flew home to spend March and April in financial support development. Crusade's policy was that each staff member should develop a financial support team to fund his or her involvement in the ministry. The process of building a support team is simple: list individuals who might be interested, make an appointment, explain your ministry and your need, and ask them to contribute. Piece o' cake, eh?

No. Building a support team takes diligence and perseverance. It involves dozens of interviews with potential supporters. One has to be graciously bold to ask for contributions and referrals. It is an opportunity to trust God completely. If you walk in that trust, the process can be enjoyable—meeting new people, hearing about their spiritual journey, and sharing the excitement of your call. I lived in that trust ... well, some of the time. At one point, my mother had to chastise me to trust God. Remarkably, all Crusade staff have their needs met in this manner.

My support target was $806 per month to cover ministry and car expenses, overheads, a significant buffer for support attrition, and a salary of $406. The average monthly gift of my supporters was twenty to thirty dollars, but there was a wide range. A widow in Roanoke contributed exactly five dollars every month.

Besides monthly support, we also raised "one-time" funding: lump sums for non-recurring expenses. In my case, the goal was $6,535 to cover training, travel, and buying a car at our ministry assignment. Six grand was a scary-large amount of money in 1978.

My support came through sources predictable or completely unexpected. Briarwood gave foundational amounts and friends, family, and work colleagues were generous.

My friends at Wesley put me in contact with a lady who might be interested in what I was doing. I didn't know her except through our mutual friends. We met and she listened carefully and asked questions. At the end, she said, "Bill, I believe the Lord is leading me to contribute $1,000." Just like that, after only knowing me for an hour!

Similarly, based on a referral, I met with a nondenominational church in another small Alabama town to which I did not have any direct ties. The church contributed $1,725. I was blown away by such generosity. Even to this day, it is humbling to think of all the people who invested in my ministry—some of whom barely knew me.

Only one person questioned my motive. An engineering manager opined that most people in ministry do it for the money. True, some hucksters are in the "religion" business, but you can usually spot their true motives. That was not my experience for anyone with a genuine heart for ministry.

The Campus Crusade pay scale was the same from top to bottom, with adjustments for the number of children if married. My Crusade salary was little more than a third of my salary working as an engineer. No one joined Campus Crusade "for the money."

International Training

In April 1978, I completed support raising and was cleared to return to San Bernardino for international training. I drove cross-country to California to join my class of Agape trainees. My mentor from Birmingham, Pat, and his wife, Linda, had become Crusade staff and they put me up until other arrangements were made.

Pat and Linda introduced me to a board game called Risk. Involving world strategy, Risk was popular with Crusade international staff. After my Bible and camera, the Risk game that I bought during training was the most useful gear I took overseas.

Agape International Training (AIT) was specific to those staff entering international work. The training was a combination of classes and ministry in cross-cultural environments. The sixty AIT candidates were divided into two training groups. One group was at a "base" in Los Angeles. The group I was assigned to was based in San Bernardino. Our classes were held at a Hispanic church, *Iglesia Bautista del Valle*.

The AIT instructors all had overseas experience, many had a military background, and most had graduate degrees and college-level teaching credentials. In addition to expertise, they were totally dedicated to equipping us for our calling.

A high priority of AIT was to simulate the stress and fatigue of immersion in foreign cultures. We would be effective in ministry only if we were comfortable living cross-culturally. As part of the cross-cultural training, AIT students lived with families of a different race.

My housing situation took longer to organize, but it was worth the wait. I lived with a black family in a ranch-style suburban home with pink rose bushes, a flagstone patio, and a nicely mowed lawn in Rialto, a suburb of San Bernardino. On Sundays, I helped wash their new Lincoln.

Coming from a modest upbringing and paying my way through college—even out on my own as an engineer—I had never lived this well. So, living far better than I was accustomed led to intense cross-cultural anxiety. OK, maybe not. I discovered I could adjust to comfort faster than washing a Lincoln Town Car.

The Jones family, my hosts, were originally from Louisiana. Their hospitality was wonderful, and we developed a warm relationship. I felt so comfortable I once took a date over to meet them. Like a good dad, Mr. Jones offered his assessment: "Bill, you sure can pick 'em."

My AIT classmates were not as well situated. For example, two of my classmates shared a double bed in a walk-in closet in Watts, a predominantly black part of Los Angeles. Oxtail soup was a favorite for dinner.

My cross-cultural experience came through attending a black church, Hebron Baptist, along with several AIT students and Sandy, a veteran Crusade trainer and a soothing encourager. Besides AIT objectives, Sandy's goal was for us to find the best burrito stand in San Bernardino.

The church service at Hebron was much more dynamic than my white church experience. Passionate sermons, shouted "amens," and hands raised in praise lit up the morning. Ladies in their wide-brimmed Sunday hats could become so jubilant they collapsed in the spirit. The ladies were aided by ushers in crisp black suits and white gloves. All the while, the long-robed choir would sing and sway. After my first church service in April, I wrote in my journal:

> *But as the afternoon wore on ... I sensed my tension in being the "odd one" [being white]. It's easy to let frustration, boredom & bewilderment lead you to uncalled for judgments.*

AIT's cross-cultural stress revealed insights on judging and provided the push to adapt. For example, over the course of AIT, I made a giant step forward in my capacity to worship. No one got drowsy in the service at Hebron; the services demanded the worshiper's full engagement. The music was phenomenal, and this white guy learned to raise his hands and sing and sway—in church, mind you.

In May, I journaled a new perspective:

This morning at church I really worshipped the Lord. Despite the noise, the unfamiliar faces, my tiredness, today I came before the Lord and praised him. Truly we don't worship in a particular building or on some mountain but in spirit and in truth [from Jesus's explanation of true worship to the woman at the well, John 4:23].

One Saturday, the Joneses visited a family member and her husband in Watts and invited me to go along. As Mr. Jones and I sat with the husband around his kitchen table, he calmly described the murder in front of his house the night before. I listened as he and Mr. Jones discussed how they both missed home back in the South, but they agreed blacks were accepted better in California.

I spent the return trip to Rialto wrapping my mind around this exchange. I loved the South and I had generations of family there. It was home in every sense of the word, but I realized now that my experience was not universal. In the 1970s, a black man could find the culture more accepting two thousand miles from his birthplace. So much so that he was willing to uproot his family and start a new life far from where he was raised.

Gaining an understanding of a black man's point of view was more than a useful perspective for a missionary. It was a serious adjustment to my ability to practice agape love.

A critical aspect of AIT was how we received cross-cultural insights. It's difficult to form a deep level of understanding of another person without living in each other's spaces. A key to understanding is to walk in the other man's shoes. Obvious when you think about it, but it takes effort. Shallow relationships can be satisfying and numbing.

Ministry

AIT ministry training consisted of methods to fulfill Jesus's final words on earth, the Great Commission:

> Therefore go and make disciples of all nations, baptizing them in the name of the Father and of the Son and of the Holy Spirit, and teaching them to observe everything I have commanded you. (Matthew 28:19-20)

Crusade's ministry strategy emphasized evangelism, small group discipleship, local church involvement, and community-wide "momentum" events. The strategy had a goal of multiplication, that is, not only to make converts to Christ but to equip and encourage these converts to also share the good news. This was in accord with the apostle Paul's teaching to his understudy, Timothy: "And the things you have heard me say in the presence of many witnesses entrust to reliable men who will also be qualified to teach others" (2 Timothy 2:2).

AIT ministry training was hands-on and aggressive. The intent was to learn by having an impact on the community around our training bases. For the first seven weeks of AIT, we had an outreach in the local community every Saturday. We used door-to-door religious surveys to talk to anyone who would listen about Jesus Christ.

Was this intimidating? Oh no, it was way beyond mere intimidation. We were as nervous as a long-tailed cat in a rocking-chair shop. Our trainers, however, had years of experience and patiently walked us through the process. With repetition, came confidence: by the end of the seven weeks, we could deliver the message of *The Four Spiritual Laws* with poise in just about any situation.

During the second seven weeks of AIT, contacts made in the first seven weeks were encouraged to join small groups. The members of these small groups were trained to create new groups.

In summary, the goals of AIT ministry training were to make contacts, form small groups, train group members, spin off new groups, involve churches, and sponsor a large momentum event, all in less than four months. We did not fulfill all the goals—for example, seven weeks is a short time to establish and train a small group. But the stretch to reach the goals accelerated the growth of our skills.

For AIT trainees who had been a part of a Crusade program in college, the training was a refinement of a familiar process. I was, of course, a practicing heathen through most of my college years and never darkened the door of a Campus Crusade meeting. So, for me, this was all new. In a way, being immersed in Crusade training was as cross-cultural as singing and swaying in church.

Kenya

The *Agape Movement Fact Sheet* stated that teams would be formed with up to ten members of similar vocational backgrounds. (My ultimate team would break the mold with fourteen members and five different types of vocations.) The San Bernardino AIT base formed a team of engineers. In late April, I noted in my journal:

> *After the leadership presentations, Agape people hung around and we had a question and answer session. A manager from Africa indicated the engineering team will go to Kenya and be working in a supervisory role. Also, he said the tentativeness of our assignments was based on our performance at AIT ("the ball is in your court").*
>
> *Suddenly felt like a not-so-important cog in a huge transmission.... I sensed myself in a nebulous ministry with nothing quite clear.*

The manager made the assignment sound less certain than I was expecting. But working overseas is chock-full of "nebulous" situations in which uncertainty can give birth to complaining. Instead of reacting to a muddled future like those without hope, we can trust "that you, O God, are strong, and that you, O Lord, are loving" (Psalm 62:11-12).

Tijuana

To further our cross-cultural experience, AIT included two week-long trips to Tijuana, Mexico. We stayed at Hotel Antonieta, a typical hotel where Mexicans stayed. It was well clear of the tourist district.

The street noise from late-rising Tijuanans often lasted way past our bedtimes. Late one boisterous evening, my classmate Ann leaned out her second-floor window, which was open because of the heat, and yelled at the top of her lungs, *"Silencio por favor!"* It's amazing how lack of sleep can bring that long-forgotten high school Spanish right back to the forefront of the cerebrum.

In the South, Ann's frustration would have prompted an earnest, "Bless her heart." (Spoken with a shake of the slightly tilted head, and with hands on the hips. Ask any Southern mom to demonstrate.)

Crossing the street in Tijuana was a death-defying feat. Potholes and pedestrians were accorded the same attention. Flashing traffic lights hung above the intersections, but the signals seemed to be more like suggestions. Cars pulled up, gunned their engines, and roared through like Saturday night in Daytona.

We ordered food in quaint diner-type restaurants where no English was to be seen or heard. At one breakfast, I considered ordering *huevos naranja* until I realized that it was poached eggs over oranges (yuck).

Our primary objective in Tijuana was to practice language-learning techniques. AIT's method, *Language Acquisition Made Practical* (LAMP), worked for any language. It's built around tape recording a native speaker repeating a phrase, such as, "I want eggs and bacon, please." Then we practiced repeating the phrase until we had it memorized. LAMP reproduced inflections and accents so well that we were often confused with native speakers.

Another objective of our Tijuana trips was to talk to people about Jesus. We ran into communications barriers that we later encountered in Africa. I recorded in my journal:

> *Experienced a double communication barrier as we attempted to share Christ with a Mexican who knew "poco" English. Not only did we have to make sure he understood our English but also if he understood spiritually the message we were trying to get across.*

Homesickness

AIT also gave us our first case of the occupational disease of missionaries—homesickness, that melancholy feeling often accompanied by a lump in the area of the heart. Even though we were still in the States, something about being a thousand miles from home and surrounded by the unfamiliar could bring it on.

Homesickness, if left to fester, can distract from the mission and steal the messenger's joy. It has no vaccine, but we found that correspondence from home and the fellowship of teammates were a balm. Whenever stricken by homesickness, we applied these liberally as an ointment for the soul.

Chapter 5

THE TEAM

In late July, I sent a postcard to my parents with a major announcement.

> *We just found out today that we have a new assignment! It's a new country that just gained its independence from South Africa called BOPHUTHATSWANA. We're real excited …*

Contractual negotiations with the Kenyan government had broken down, but the Bophuthatswana government needed our professional skills and was anxious for us to come. To relieve our knotted tongues, we adopted the locals' nickname for the "new country:" *Bophu* (bow poo).

The AIT engineering team was merged with a group of teachers, sports instructors, health professionals, and agricultural advisors, most of whom we knew from AIT. We researched our new assignment and found that Bophu was the homeland for people of the *Tswana* (SWA na) tribe. It consisted of six separate regions, each about the size of a US county, that were all embedded within South Africa. Although South Africa had large modern cities, Bophu held farming towns and rural villages. The nature of the land was grassland with mild weather.

We also learned that when the South African government declared Bophu independent, every member of the Tswana tribe, all two million—whether currently living within the homeland or not—automatically had their South African citizenship revoked and they became citizens of Bophu. Was this controversial? Oh yes, but it was only one of many controversies. Throughout South Africa, the atmosphere was tinged with a smoldering crisis.

The Smoldering Land

The Republic of South Africa of 1978 was a troubled country. The minority white government was desperately trying to hold at bay the majority black population under its policy of *apartheid* (uh PAR tate), a Dutch-derived word meaning "apart-ness." Meanwhile, black leaders were desperately trying to gain political control and a full share in the South African economy.

The racial makeup of South Africa was unique to the continent. In most sub-Saharan African countries, the white percentage was a single digit or merely an asterisk, but in South Africa, whites made up 17 percent of the population. The Dutch-descended whites, the *Afrikaners* (off free CON ers), traced their lineage back over three hundred years in Africa. They were sometimes referred to as the "white tribe." South Africa also had significant percentages of mixed race and Asian peoples.

In granting "independence," the government of South Africa was simply transferring land historically reserved for black tribes to governments led by tribal leaders. Homelands spun off from South Africa did not have unfettered power over government functions like taxes or a court system. Instead, they were in a "mother may I" arrangement with the parent South African government. Bophu did not even control its borders, which would have been impractical anyway because its regions had territory added or excised on an ongoing basis. For these reasons, the independent homelands were not recognized as sovereign nations by other countries and had been spurned by the United Nations.

Under apartheid, whites were forbidden to live in black areas of South Africa. For example, the small town of Mafikeng was designated for whites, and its much larger suburb *Montshiwa* (mont SHE wuh) was designated for blacks. Somewhere in between the two was the unmarked border of Bophu.

The segregation law did not apply within the pseudo-independent homelands. So, the "independence" enabled us to live side by side with the Tswana in Montshiwa. We were among the few whites to live in a black area in all of South Africa.

The creation of independent homelands was looked on by some as a fair and final future. For others it was only tolerable to provide breathing room to work out a better solution. And by still others, it was kowtowing and surrendering to callous oppression.

From a ministry viewpoint, the development of the homelands provided entry to Bophu with the message of hope.

The original assignment to Kenya had never felt quite real. This new assignment felt all too real; it felt like a challenge impossible without the company of God.

July 27 (San Bernardino Mountains)

I can see some of the future problems too, of being in a land [South Africa] that oppresses the group we'll be working with and being white myself. It will take diplomacy, tact, love, and prayer. Thank you God that it's a challenge I'll have to believe you for.

The Last Goodbye

The ministry portion of AIT had not seemed productive despite many hours invested in the community. However, in our last outreach, our "momentum event," many attendees indicated they had prayed to ask Christ to come into their lives. Some stayed afterward, as long as two hours, to discuss Christianity's effects on everyday life. It was a powerful sendoff to the mission field.

July 29 (Rialto)

Today I got checked out for A.I.T., today I bought a [huge] suitcase to take to Africa, today Mr. Jones told me how much he enjoyed having me here this summer.

It's been so incredible; never have I learned and experienced so much in so short a time.

We had a formal graduation for AIT on August 2. Afterward, we packed up our newly minted skills and said goodbye to hosts, teachers, and classmates. I left with satisfaction that I had been equipped for my calling as much as was humanly possible in the span of one summer.

At home in Alabama, I sold my car and donated my drums to Briarwood. I signed a power-of-attorney so my dad could represent me in any legal matter. And then began a more emotional round of goodbyes.

I would be away from home, family, and country, without any interim return, for a full two years. I had my excitement to carry me, but my family, particularly my mom, did not have that crutch. As a parent now, I can imagine their anxiety as I packed my bags for another world.

September 2 (Roanoke)

Today is THE day.

Inside my emotions run the gamut from fear to excitement. The TV special last night [a documentary on South Africa] impressed me again with the magnitude of the problem in South Africa. Yet excitement persists: what an adventure! ... I rely on the lesson of this summer, "it is required in servants that a man be found faithful."

As I packed last nite and as the TV show went on, I realized I may well return empty handed and I turned all my goods over to the Lord. I'm not counting on bringing any of what I have home. Except myself, but that last important item I also put in his hands ...

My parents drove me to the Atlanta airport with my huge California suitcase and my huge dreams. My mom's now-healthy heart was strong enough for the two-hour drive. My bags were checked, my passport was cleared, and my ticket was clipped. I turned for one last wave goodbye, then walked down the ramp to Africa.

Chapter 6

THE ARRIVAL

It was the start of fall in North America, but the beginning of spring when my teammates and I crossed the equator to enter the Southern Hemisphere. In the spring in South Africa, a crimson wildflower called protea is in bloom. According to tradition, the protea flower represents hope. Acrossced the grassland of the central South African plains, the dull straw color of winter gives way to a vibrant green. Acacia thorn trees begin sprouting yellow blossoms with a sweet and pleasant, or *lekker*, fragrance. Africa was bestowing on the sojourners a proper African welcome.

From Atlanta, I had flown to Philadelphia where I joined my teammates. From Philly, we had flown to London overnight and then waited an interminable time in Heathrow Airport's baggage claim for our luggage to be located. That evening, we boarded a second overnight flight, from Heathrow to Nairobi, Kenya. After refueling, the flight continued from Nairobi to Johannesburg.

We arrived on the afternoon of Monday, September 4, 1978, at the modern international airport in Johannesburg. We had been traveling between fifty to sixty hours from our different hometowns. We were dead tired, but our feet now touched Africa.

Gathering our baggage, we cleared customs and passport control. The airport was crowded, and the officials kept saying, "Carry on, carry on," which was confusing until in my jet-lag stupor I realized they simply meant "get moving."

We then found the commuter airline for the flight to Mafikeng. The airline said we could only take one small bag each and they would deliver the rest of our baggage over the next few days. We watched our bags being trundled back into the terminal and wondered if we would ever see them again. We did. (Miraculously, all of our thirty-four pieces of luggage made it through three plane changes and fifteen thousand air miles.)

The pilot of the commuter flight avoided the goat and landed us safely on the grass runway at Mafikeng. A Bophu government official was on hand to formally greet us, along with John, the leader of our Crusade team. His wife, Lynn, had stayed home to cook our first meal in Africa.

The day after we arrived, still groggy from our travels, we had a meeting with Lucas Mangope, the president of Bophu. He welcomed us warmly and told us how important it was for us to help the Tswana people. President Mangope's calmness belied the fact that he was under intense pressure to improve the quality of life of the Bophu citizens. He had taken harsh criticism for his decision to accept the offer of "independence" for Bophu. Now he needed to show results.

I wrote in my journal:

September 9

Have surely felt awed by the great opportunity and challenge we find ourselves in. I remember the chart [from training] that showed the first month or so as a real "high." But I know as the newness wears off it will be hard to retain the desire to do the utmost at everything. Lynn said something important, "Do not confuse enthusiasm with motivation." Good advice.

John's car broke down later that first week. We pushed it to the side of the road while someone went to borrow another car. This was our first experience of many with missionary flexing. But it was a beautiful, cool spring night with a star-filled sky. In the distance was the faint chugging of locomotives, coal-fired steam engines, working in the rail yard in Mafikeng. This soothing sound was our background music on any evening outdoors.

The Americans Move In

The contracts for our government jobs would begin on October 2, about four weeks away. We spent September settling in—renting post office boxes at the Montshiwa post office, completing applications for work visas, and applying for Bophu driver's licenses using our International Driver's Licenses. We opened bank accounts at Barclays or Standard Bank of South Africa and transferred money from our Bank of America accounts in California.

The unit of currency of the Republic of South Africa is the "rand." The exchange rate of a US dollar to one rand, when we first arrived, was about $1.15 to R1.00. Bophu never issued a separate currency, so all of our transactions were in rand.

The team was divided up into temporary housing. Several teammates and I stayed with a Canadian couple who had a nice brick home in the hospital housing compound. Ben and Cathy were serving Bophu independent of any mission or charitable agency; they came on their own to fulfill their call. Ben was a surgeon at *Bophelong* (BOW pay long), the Tswana hospital located in Montshiwa. Their home was a North American oasis for us.

The long-term housing plan was for all of us to receive government housing. The Bophu government was building five- and six-room concrete block houses in row after row along dusty, rock-strewn, unpaved, and unnamed "streets" in Montshiwa. With indoor plumbing and electricity, they were nice (speaking as a bachelor). They were painted pastel colors resembling Florida beach houses.

The new Montshiwa houses were a significant upgrade from standard-issue black housing. The typical South African government-supplied house was a four-room matchbox without electricity and with outhouses and a community water spigot for plumbing. Housing for blacks was in chronic short supply, and shantytowns sprang up near the large South African cities. The forceful clearing of these camps by the police was a frequent news item.

Phones were rare in Montshiwa—the Montshiwa phonebook had maybe 100 listings out of ninety thousand residents. We didn't pursue obtaining service (who would've called us?) even though there were poles and cable strung in our backyard. John and Lynn eventually had phone service at their house, after a four-month wait, and we made our calls home from there. In 1978, calling overseas from Africa involved making a reservation with the local operator and then hanging by the phone for a couple of hours till the call was connected. Therefore, the parties had to have an agreed time scheduled weeks in advance by mail. I didn't call home often; international calls cost two dollars per minute.

Our initial grocery-shopping sortie was a voyage of discovery. Products tended to be similar but not quite what we were used to. For example, milk was sold in plastic jugs like at home but had cream floating on top of the milk. The picture on the raisin box looked the same as the US equivalent, but the product inside tasted more like sweet gravel. Meat had a cutting of parsley or a slice of cucumber under the clear wrapping to certify freshness. White bread was expensive, so we bought brown, unsliced government-subsidized bread for twenty-five cents per loaf.

On one shopping safari, we rejoiced to find cans of Minute Maid orange juice in the back of the frozen foods section. Although the packaging was the same, the taste was lip-pursing sour. We found pasta but no taco shells. We learned to like mangoes instead of apples and guavas instead of peaches. The local Checkers store, a branch of the largest grocery chain in southern Africa, came to be our favorite. Actually, it was everyone's favorite because it was the only full-sized grocery store in Mafikeng or Montshiwa.

The Hangout

Buying a reliable vehicle was a key part of settling in, and each of us had raised $1,500 for this purchase. Each household had a vehicle: Married couple Alex and Cindy bought a small station wagon, roommates Bonnie and Ann bought a compact four-door sedan, and roommates Steve and Duane bought a two-door coupe. Roommates Joe, Mike, and Bill went in together to buy a low-slung Porsche Carrera.

A Porsche? Not quite—but the type of vehicle we should buy was quite a debate. The suggestion for the three of us to buy a Volkswagen bus—I don't know who to blame, or to thank—came up as a practical alternative to a car. In Africa and many other parts of the world, the Volkswagen bus is called a *kombi* (COM bee), short for the German word, *kombinationsfahrzeug*, which means "combined purpose vehicle" (an American might say multipurpose vehicle). In the US, it's associated with hippies and flower children. But in Africa, a kombi is a mechanical workhorse, an upgrade from the donkey cart.

For us single guys, buying a kombi was like buying a minivan: practical and roomy but so uncool. But in the end, the three of us took one for the team. We pooled our funds and shopped for a kombi.

One area in which AIT did not provide a manual was how to fend off the hyper-aggressive South African car dealers. Their sales tactics would cause a high-pressure American car salesman to hide his face in shame.

(Author's note: If no location is noted, the journal entry was written in Montshiwa.)

September 28

Wildest experience lately was the car hunt. Contacted a dealership Monday in Mafikeng about a Kombi & a Volkswagen Passat (for the girls). They went nuts calling all over to get "good cars for the Americans." But they didn't have what we wanted. That nite however their contact in Lichtenburg brought 6 (six) cars to Montshiwa for us to look at!

The six used vehicles were brought sixty-five kilometers (forty miles) for our inspection. The salesmen parked them in a row facing our house with the headlights shining through the front windows. The inside of the house was lit up like a police raid.

"Look how good the brake pedal is," one of the salesmen exclaimed. In Africa, the wear of the brake pedal was thought to provide a deep revelation on the innermost mechanical condition of the vehicle. I recorded in my journal that during a test drive I talked about Jesus with the salesman, and he turned out to be a Jesus follower.

On another day, we traveled to the nearby town of Lichtenburg to explore other dealerships. Our reputations as kombi seekers had preceded us to other towns.

> *We did go on to Lichtenburg to look for a car. Everybody seemed to know us, "the Americans looking for a Kombi." One guy even pulled up beside us as we walked down the street asking us to come to his place.*

It was late October when we located a used kombi for sale in the small town of Vryburg, about fifty kilometers (thirty miles) away. The dealer did not need to be a salesman as it was obvious to us that this was God's provision as soon as we saw it. We settled upon a price, which was the amount we had raised in support, even considering the latest exchange rate.

Our 1976 Volkswagen 2000L kombi was unfailingly dependable. It never let us down. Even when the mechanic did not tighten the drain plug and the oil ran out on the road, no permanent harm resulted. It did not have four-wheel drive, but for some reason when you sat in that driver's seat you felt like the kombi could master any type of road—even a donkey-cart path. Maybe it was the roaring engine noise that made you believe it was doing its very best to please you. The kombi never got stuck, and it never bottomed out. The kombi was steady enough for bad roads, and smooth enough for good ones.

From the outside, it was nothing sleek or worthy of a second look. It was a yellow box on wheels, two-tone with a white top and the "VW" emblem on the front. The gear-shift lever was long and slender and felt like it was connected to rubber bungee cords. Shifting was more akin to stirring tapioca pudding than connecting iron gearing. Stops for "petrol"—that is, gasoline—were few and far between.

The kombi served two purposes. The first and most obvious was utilitarian transportation. It could carry a driver plus six passengers in American-style comfort, or a dozen in African-style comfort. Along with the seven seats, it had space in the way-back sufficient for plenty of luggage or cargo. It was a pickup truck, limousine, and Land Rover all in one. It was a land-going African Queen.

The second need the kombi filled was not as obvious. It satisfied a need we didn't know we had. It was large enough to be our hangout where we were close enough, for long enough, not to sulk, or be sad or homesick by ourselves; close enough to share some teasing, or a joke, and a lot of laughter.

The kombi was a veritable member of the team—maybe the most faithful member. The kombi lugged us to work and the post office every day, carried pastors and their singing congregations to revivals, wafted us across the continent from ocean to ocean, watched drive-in movies with us, and even hauled a smelly, bleating sheep to be butchered. The kombi never once complained.

As with so many of my experiences in Africa, the kombi was something ordinary that produced extraordinary results when placed in the service of Jesus.

Language 101

After settling in, language learning was a high priority. We used the LAMP process we had been taught in AIT. The name of the Tswana language is formed by adding the prefix Se to the name of the tribe to form *Setswana*. As in any language 101 course, we first learned the basic Setswana greetings and introductory phrases. As we had experienced in Mexico, the LAMP method enabled us to sound exactly like a native speaker, that is, for the phrases we had worked on.

When we tried out our phrases with the Tswana people, we received a delighted smile, joyous clapping, and then a rapid string of Setswana as the listener expressed wonderment at how quickly we had become fluent (at least we thought that was what was being said). To forestall disillusionment when we couldn't continue a conversation, we kept a phrase near at hand: *Ke itse fela go le kalo,* meaning, "I only know this little bit." My October journal noted:

> *The Tswana people are overjoyed at the limited knowledge of Setswana we have; quite impressed that whites are learning their language.*

Language learning opened doors by demonstrating our sincerity. The validation of our intentions was just as important to our ministry as the improvement in communication.

Learning Setswana is more difficult than learning, say, Spanish, because English and Setswana have no common words or similarity in structure or grammar. Setswana was spelled phonetically, but some of the letters—"tsw," for example—represent a consonant not found in English.

Bophu had three official languages: Setswana, English, and Afrikaans. Official Bophu documents were translated into all three languages. Tswana school children had classes in all three, and public notices and signs were in two or three languages. This seemed inefficient, particularly the burden on students' time, but then I was not brought up in a multilingual culture. Europeans typically grow up learning two or more languages.

Afrikaans originated with the Dutch colonists. A significant portion of the Afrikaans vocabulary are words picked up from English, German, and French immigrants, and from the *Khoikhoi* (coy coy) tribe, also known as *Hottentot*. Since some of us worked with Afrikaners in our vocational roles, we ended up learning fragments of that language as well. Like the Tswana, the Afrikaners were pleased we were making the attempt.

Because of Africa's embracing cultures, the origin of individual names was all over the map, or more accurately, *from* all over the map. Some Tswana had an English first name, such as a Biblical personality, and some had Afrikaans names. Afrikaners generally had a Dutch, German, or French-derived name. But some had an English first name or surname, or both.

The Tswana language uses prefixes and suffixes like Latin. A quirk to this language is that many of the prefixes for proper nouns begin with the letter "M," for example, Mafikeng, Montshiwa, and Mangope. Roughly half of the listings in the Bophu phone book were "M" names.

South Africans of any race or tribe used an Afrikaans expression that sounded like the Scottish word "loch," as in Loch Lomond, but with the "l" dropped, that is, "-och." It was spoken as a guttural word, on the cusp of a gargle, from the back of the throat. An attempt at a phonetic English spelling is *auk* (but don't forget "-och"). Auk was used for regret, disdain, disbelief, even modesty, and certainly surprise.

To add some precision, auk could be accompanied with *nie* (KNEE uh), meaning no, or sometimes *mon*, meaning man (I think), to form *auk nie* or *auk mon*. For particularly colorful situations, all three were used: *auk nie mon*. These expressions came in quite handy.

The Maytag and the Hulk

Soon after we landed, a neighbor of John and Lynn's, who had heard through the community grapevine that there were American engineers in town, asked the mechanical engineer—me—to come to their house to repair their washing machine. This appliance was a novelty in Montshiwa.

I dutifully answered the call; however, as a bachelor, my technical experience with washing machines ended when I put the quarter in the slot at the laundromat. Sadly, the neighbor's machine did not have a quarter slot. Shaking my head in my most professional manner, I applied a newly learned phrase: *ga ke itse* (ha kay EAT say), meaning, "I don't know." I chuckled to think that I had flown across the Atlantic to be an unsuccessful Maytag repairman.

On another day, I was at John and Lynn's house when the front door was pounded loudly. We opened to meet Mr. *Botha* (bow tuh) from the Bophu Department of Works. Mr. Botha was a white Afrikaner with rugged features who somewhat resembled the Hulk. A former rugby player, he was a huge man and filled the frame of the door. He was to be my first supervisor at the Department of Works and wanted to know when I was coming to work; he said we had much to do. Mr. Botha would have to wait a few weeks until our contracts started.

Mr. Botha was a type of government employee called *seconded* (suh CON did). To assist the fledgling Bophu government, the white South African government lent civil servants to Bophu government agencies. So even though he was working in the Bophu government ranks, Botha's paycheck came from the South African government. The seconded officials were experienced in how government bureaucracy was intended to work, and they carried a level of technical skills.

The Bull Ox

Mr. Botha, his first language being Afrikaans, spoke a deep, guttural English; his pronunciation of my name came out as "Bull" instead of Bill. My teammates took to calling me Bull. At one of our first ministry opportunities, I demonstrated that I was indeed as dumb as an ox.

Went to church yesterday at the hostel of the local high school, gave my testimony as did Mike. Ben gave a short evangelistic sermon. The students were very friendly and very open; talked for about an hour with some of them afterward.

The audience was a large group of around 250 students. Our talks were in English, without a translator to Setswana, but the messages seemed to be getting across to the students. In the question-and-answer session after the program, the students asked us about our views on the issue of "girlfriends and boyfriends." I naively thought that the question was referring to juvenile relationships amounting to hand-holding, and I was about to answer in that vein, when my teammate Joe jumped up to address the audience. His answer cut quickly and directly to the Biblical stand on sexual morality. Joe had discerned correctly that the question was about intimate relationships. The relationship translated as "girlfriend and boyfriend" in English was about much more than hand-holding.

We later learned that it were not uncommon for a man to insist that the woman of his affections demonstrate she could have a baby, or two, before he would be interested in marriage. Because of a poor translation, we almost missed the opportunity to take a stand against this practice.

Conversations always seemed to touch on the political situation. Sometimes this was a distraction, and sometimes it opened doors.

Two fellows linked up with me as I went to the Post Office. Tswana teenagers, both 16, nice guys, followed me all over town. Hard to communicate, our accents don't complement each other. Briefly shared how to become a Jesus follower, very difficult to judge the response. Again, political views, i.e., resentments, surfaced briefly.

We were a curiosity; a white living in a black township was unique in 1978 South Africa. The Tswana were naturally curious as to why we chose to live this way and why we had come to their country. It was a natural flow to go from the political situation, to our motives for coming, to our belief in God.

However, having someone's attention did not mean the message was conveyed. Early on, I had an opportunity to talk about Jesus with a young Tswana man using an evangelistic tract. One question in the tract was on assurance of salvation and asked rhetorically, "Would Jesus lie to you?" Eager to please, my smiling listener said, "Yes." Obviously, I was not getting the message across. *What was going on?*

In general, people did not want to admit they could not understand enough English to follow a conversation. When a person did not understand a question, particularly from someone in authority, the default answer to the question was "yes." Besides the Tswana, I had a similar experience with an Afrikaans-speaking white who knew little English. In a September journal entry I noted: "People we are ministering to often give the answers they think you want. We must be more careful to discern where they are spiritually."

Getting a message across required slow and careful pronunciation plus gestures and sometimes role-play. Communication was possible but laden with pitfalls for the unsuspecting linguistic ox.

Chapter 7

THE SONS

In late September, Mike and I moved out of Ben and Cathy's house and into the home of a Tswana married couple: *Khumo* (COO mow) and Faith. We would stay in this home for almost two months, and then the plan was for the two of us plus Joe to rent one of the government houses under construction. In our temporary housing, Mike and I shared a bedroom and bathroom. For a black township in South Africa, it was palatial.

Khumo and Faith were in their mid-thirties, well-educated, and they spoke perfect English. Khumo was a serious, no-nonsense sort of guy. He was a chief in the Tswana tribe and held a senior position in the Bophu government where he spent long hours. Though Khumo and Faith lived in town, he frequently talked about his love for farming.

Faith was a social worker, a role for which her demeanor and communication skills were a natural fit. Always smiling, Faith had the gift of hospitality. However, she admitted to us later that when Khumo had first mentioned to her that two young American "chaps" needed accommodations, she was troubled due to her experience living under apartheid. The thought of whites, not to mention foreigners, living in her home was unnerving. She didn't think such an arrangement could possibly work.

But Faith quickly warmed to us. She later quoted the saying that "a stranger is a friend you don't know." She began to help us with cultural and language tutoring. She and Khumo were frequently stretching us with new Setswana words and phrases.

Faith was also a delightful Jesus follower, and we had many Bible and Christian life discussions. For example, Faith felt the disciple Thomas was being honest about his doubt. And she believed the Lord could teach us a lot from the book of Exodus because she said, "The children of Israel were going places with God."

Faith came to refer to us as her sons, and she admitted that she and Khumo liked to take us on outings so they could show us off. And she indeed mothered us, saying how much she missed us when we were away. In the mornings, when schedules allowed, she prepared breakfast for Khumo and the two of us, and we listened to the somber, British-accented BBC announcer read the news before we all went to work.

Faith taught us about the South African staple food, made from ground corn and served at almost every meal, called *mielie pap* (me LEE pop). It was frequently served with a tomato sauce and, as Faith demonstrated to us, it could be accompanied by spinach or corned beef. Spinach served alone is sometimes mixed with peanut butter, as Faith said, "to make it tasty." (Mielie pap was simply a stiff version of grits, the South's famous side dish, though Southerners garnish it with red-eye gravy.)

Faith explained that she was given her name because, after waiting nine years, her parents were depending on "faith" for a child. Her father said that as a child she was "as small as my thumb," so her nickname growing up was "Faith, my thumb."

The Kicker

Khumo and Faith took us on several enlightening outings. On one jaunt, we visited members of one of their families who lived on a farm. As we got to know the family, Khumo went into the kitchen and brought out a serving tray with a teapot, milk, and sugar to hold before each person so they could make themselves a cup of tea. At one point, as he went around the room from person to person, he turned to Mike and me and remarked, "Are your arms broken?" From this, we learned that good tea manners dictated that the younger members of a party—in this case, Mike and me—should serve the older, which that day happened to be everyone else in the room.

Khumo spoke his mind, which was unusual in a culture that often bore affronts in stoic silence. His candor was instructive for the two of us, while the kindness of Faith was a reassurance.

Another outing was a social event for high-level government officials. It was hosted by a senior administrative official, who was seconded to the Bophu government from the South African government, and his wife. This was an eye-opening evening.

September 22

Tonight, provided a unique insight into the dynamics of Afrikaner/Tswana relations, of apartheid and of the strange situations and ironies it produces. We had dinner at the home of a high-level white administrator, an Afrikaner; we went with Khumo and Faith. Several Tswana senior officials and their wives were there ...

As the party began the men sat outside and imbibed ... the administrator is fluent in Tswana. He was making much of being a citizen of Bophu, that they were all friends, etc. There were several comments he made toward us [Mike and me]; about being men or we'd have to be shipped home, stress on us learning Tswana before we started working for the government.

We had a delicious meal that included impala, great desserts, etc. The conversation was wild, sliding from Tswana to Afrikaans to English and mixing the three. Subjects were from the price of liquor in Mafikeng and Montshiwa to making the administrator a chief.

The most exciting part of the evening was as we drove home and Khumo & Faith explained the underlying things going on.

As Khumo and Faith explained the situation, the irony was rich. The underlying philosophy of apartheid was to strictly separate the races. Yet to make the homeland successful, the South African government provided white seconded officials that were embedded throughout the Bophu government. But in so doing, the seconded whites ended up even closer to blacks than ever before, which was the exact thing the entire process was meant to prevent. Continuing the previous journal entry:

> *The kicker: Khumo said the administrator had taken him aside and asked him why Americans were needed here, could not South Africans accomplish the same? Khumo's straight forward answer is beautiful; Bophu is not just a multi-racial country it is a non-racial country. They will accept whoever wants to help them as long as there were no strings. I am indeed a sojourner in a very foreign land!*

It was important for us to understand that although we came to Bophu for a ministry, we had access to the country due to our vocational skills and not everyone thought that we were necessary.

Customs and Culture

Because of his long work hours, we saw less of Khumo, but I think he also enjoyed having us around and learning about these strange alien Americans. At the end of our stay, we bought them a large starving-artist sort of painting—a pastoral scene featuring cattle on a farm. We meant to appeal to Khumo's love of farming, and I think he smiled a bit at that. Just a thumb-sized bit.

Besides Faith's tutoring, Khumo also taught us about African customs. Khumo explained that the role of the eldest son carries more authority and responsibilities in African culture than in Western culture. The eldest son is lawgiver, judge, and breadwinner.

I recorded Khomo's explanation of African social structure in my journal.

> *Very enlightening discussion with Khumo when we returned home. He explained the chieftain system. It's a hereditary position, so he decides, but he is not an absolute authoritarian, and must do as the majority of people want. There is a hierarchy of leadership, each level is hereditary. A man might have wealth but he is not ascribed respect for his wealth, but only for his relative level.*

Ability too is not a factor, no one can "outshine" those of the level above them. True, the chief or elders may put their abilities to good use but it is the [next higher level] chief or elder that will get the credit; the person will shine thru the proper chain of command.

The system is not rigid anymore, Khumo would never have been allowed to leave the clan homestead in the "olden days." The clan or family is extended in the sense that even 10th cousins have as many rights in Khumo's house as his sister or brother. Everything is shared, all are cared for, illegitimate kids or old folks are not sent away to homes. Khumo stressed how very close the families are.

An aside: The above journal entry went on to say, "It's a very different social structure and priority system from the West. A man is not considered independent and wealth is not a measure of status."

In broad (not exhaustive) terms, Western culture tended to use financial means—that is, insurance, savings or taxes—to cover sickness, old age, and calamities like disabilities. Parents might even believe that the following generation should not be burdened with their infirmities. In African culture—at least in traditional African society—time and resources were expended to maintain broad family and community ties that filled in for life's insecurities.

Both cultures had the same societal problems, but the contrast in how these problems were addressed was huge. In this and other cultural areas, it is natural for different values to develop. But cultural values often become a lens for *judging* other people. For example, I heard whites express disdain at the seeming lack of concern for material assets in African society, and I heard Africans express disdain at the materialism of Western society.

How much rejection of others is rooted in these contrasts? How much fear of forced change is engendered? What if two groups were the same race, yet had strong differences in cultural values: some European immigrants to America, for example? Is rejection because of cultural values distinguishable from "racism"?

On Grief

While living with Khumo and Faith, we attended a Tswana funeral that I described in a letter home.

> *This morning we went to a funeral for a young government official killed in a car wreck last week. It was a big deal. Started at 8:00 and the service ran to about 10:30. Many hymns, speeches, etc. even one by President Mangope. Then the whole party went to the graveyard, at least a thousand people, minimum. The roads were jammed. Everybody stayed till the casket was completely buried and stones piled on the grave. Then everyone went back to the house for a ceremonial handwashing and a small meal ...*

Khumo and Faith did not have children, but Faith shared with us that they had two sons who were now in heaven. Faith recounted how one of her sons passed away. When the child was still a baby, he became sick, and she and Khumo took a train to reach a doctor. Few doctors would treat a black baby, and the closest was some distance from where they lived at the time. While on the way, the baby passed away in her arms. Faith told Khumo, then she put the baby in a box. At the next station, they changed trains to return home and have a funeral for the child. They could do nothing more.

From this story, I better understood the stern heart of Khumo, while marveling at the peaceful heart of Faith.

It was a deeply enriching experience to live in the home of Khumo and Faith, but we always knew it was short term. On Sunday, November 5, Mike and I sadly hugged Faith goodbye—such a precious, beautiful Jesus follower. We shook hands with Khumo in the African manner that one uses with a chief: With my left hand I held the wrist of my right hand, and my right hand was extended to grasp the chief's right hand. Simultaneously I bowed my head at the shoulders.

Then we picked up our bags, joined Joe, and moved into our brand-new government house: the one with the number 2293 stenciled in black on the lavender door, located on another of the dusty, unnamed streets of Montshiwa.

Chapter 8

THE ENGINEERS

Our ministry to Bophu was like an open book: On one side was the page with our spiritual ministry of evangelism, training, and multiplication, and on the opposite page was our service to meet physical needs. In practical terms, we spent as much or more of our waking hours on the physical problems of the country as we did in spiritual ministry.

On October 2, the nine new recruits reported to government offices to begin our vocational work assignments. Bonnie and Cindy (Alex's wife) reported as teachers and Ann and Joe as sports and physical-education instructors. Duane and Steve reported to a nearby prison farm to serve as agricultural advisors. The three engineers—Alex, Mike, and I—reported to the Department of Works.

Mr. *Masibi* (muh SEE bee) was the head of the Department of Works. Secretary Masibi reported to the minister of works, a cabinet-level position, who reported to President Mangope. Masibi was in effect the chief operations officer for all of the government's physical plant and infrastructure. The Bophu government was engaged in improving key quality of life areas such as housing, utilities, roads, and electrification. An entire city of government buildings named *Mmabatho* (mah BAH two), "mother of the people," was being built adjacent to the township of Montshiwa. Masibi's job was broad and heavy.

Masibi was a good man for this challenge. He was an outstanding leader: intelligent, personable, and authoritative yet unassuming. He gained our respect and inspired our desire to serve. We encountered few other executives of any nationality as well-balanced and capable.

Besides his leadership, Masibi was remarkable because of his cross-cultural skills. He was able to effectively communicate abstract ideas to both Africans and Americans. One of his introductory comments was to note, tongue-in-cheek, that since America had put a man on the moon, he was expecting great things of American engineers in Africa. He told us that we had our book knowledge of engineering, but in Bophu, we would learn human engineering. And that we did.

Masibi took opportunities to teach us about the Tswana condition. He once noted in our presence to a young Tswana quietly seated in his reception area that he could wait a little longer since "we are from a people used to waiting." His use of English indicated the message was meant for us. He had a sly wit. He once quoted the adage that all men are heads of their households, "when their wives allow it."

Our workplace was the Imperial Reserve, the administrative office buildings left over from the period 1885 to 1966, when the British Empire controlled the Bechuanaland Protectorate, now the country of Botswana. The Imperial Reserve was a frontier outpost of the British Empire at its peak. If those walls could have talked, the stories of explorers and exploiters, opportunists and imperialists, chiefs and commanders, and brave, faithful missionaries would have been fascinating.

The offices were old but serviceable if one didn't mind function-over-form. They consisted of narrow buildings of masonry with stuccoed plaster walls and corrugated roofing. The buildings formed squares around courtyards, and the offices opened onto a covered walkway similar to the design of an American motel. The offices used ceramic convection heaters in the winter and crank-out windows and electric fans in the summer. Plenty of ancient cypress trees provided shade. We dressed appropriately, and with central South Africa's moderate climate, our offices were comfortable.

The government office attire was a coat, white shirt, and tie. However, a dress convention called a "safari suit" was allowed: an outfit similar to the leisure suit of the 1970s but with short sleeves and short pants. Knee socks were a required part of the ensemble. Even Masibi wore a safari suit.

We had intense meetings involving millions of rand with consultants, government officials, and their minions all arrayed in shorts and knee socks. If your workplace dress code is too formal, try unplugging the air conditioning.

Starting Work

When Alex, Mike, and I joined the Department of Works, we raised the number of degreed engineers directly employed by the Bophu government to three. Due to apartheid's restrictions on education, there was not a single degreed engineer among all of Bophu's citizens—a population of some two million. The Bophu government was totally dependent on consulting engineers from South Africa and the seconded officials from the South African government. The three of us were well educated in our fields, but we had only a few years of post-bachelor-degree experience. Even so, our abilities were sorely needed as *independent* technical advisors.

October 3 (Tweespruit Hotel—Somewhere near Thaba 'Nchu)

Today, my 2nd at work, Botha and I drove down from Mafikeng to Thaba 'Nchu [located 500 kilometers, or 313 miles, south of Mafikeng].

Maybe I should start with yesterday, 1st day of work. It was vague where we were to report but we simply showed up at the Dept. of Works and somehow ended up in Mr. Pretorius' office. So, we chatted awhile, he gave some of his background—he's spent much time all over the world.

Mr. Pretorius was in charge of engineering matters, and he reported directly to Masibi. It was decided that Alex would serve as interim architect for the department and facilitate development projects. Mike would work closely with a Tswana technician to pave roads around Montshiwa and in the new town of Mmabatho. I would assist Mr. Botha on water projects such as reservoirs and distribution systems.

Botha and I traveled all over the scattered fragments of Bophu in October and November inspecting projects and coordinating with consultants and contractors. A coordination meeting is what took us to the isolated piece of Bophu named *Thaba 'Nchu* (tuh BAN chew), a long drive south of Mafikeng. Continuing the previous entry:

> *Back to the trip—waited till it came up, but gave my testimony stressing what it meant to receive Christ. Led into (or maybe it was vice versa) discussion on immorality and Christian standards. Botha was quiet and listened ...*
>
> *Right now, we're in a quaint hotel in well, somewhere. Small rooms; community bath; pub down the hall noisy with leftover patrons. Met an Englishman over dinner, 21 years in Africa, 9 in South Africa ... he remarked how strange were some of the things South Africa does while claiming to be Christian. Oh, how true!*

The political situation was inescapable, and it seemed to hang over everything like a cloud. During our trip, I shared with Botha a vague family legend that somewhere in our ancestry was an American Indian. So, if true, in South Africa I would be a person of mixed-race descent and therefore a member of a non-white racial class. I thought it would be funny, but Botha's piercing sidewise glance told me it was not. Heritage stories that were interesting anecdotes in America were deadly serious under apartheid.

Later in my term in Africa, I had a conversation with a white South African about genealogy and I had a racial insight, a walking-in-their-skin (not shoes) discernment.

> *Sat. nite as we talked about ancestors, for a moment I was ashamed of the legend that I had American Indian blood— something I'd always been proud of. I think for a moment I knew how the mixed-race Coloured people feel ...*

I wondered in this cloud-parting moment about all the ramifications if I moved to South Africa, became a citizen, and was classified as a non-white. I would be subject to job and career limits, housing and educational restrictions, and social constraints, not to mention all the day-to-day discriminations from bathrooms to buses. This insight gave me a visceral feeling for the consequences of apartheid.

In Black and White

As an outsider, I observed a tacit tension between the black Tswana and the white seconded officials, but the two groups still worked well together. The Tswana needed the expertise of the seconded officials, and the seconded officials wanted to make the homeland experiment a success. It was remarkable, given the potential under apartheid for hostility between the races, that the organization functioned (that is, as well as any government functions).

My colleagues had admirable dedication. English-speaking white, or Afrikaans-speaking white, or the black Tswana—all worked hard and to the best of their abilities. A white Afrikaans manager once chastised me for expressing, in his opinion, a less than long-term view of my role in the government.

My team and I sat squarely between two worlds. From the white officials, we received respect because we were educated Westerners, because we jumped right in and tried hard to help, and because they recognized we were giving up a great deal to be there. They looked beyond our curious decision to live in a black area and invited us to their homes for a *braaivleis*, a cookout, and to meet their families.

From the Tswana officials, we received respect because we were from a country that opposed apartheid and, again, because we were giving up a great deal to help them. The Tswana loved our acceptance of African culture, the fact that we lived in the black township, and that we were attempting to learn their language. They also invited us to their feasts and family gatherings.

Both races expressed a touching acceptance, friendliness, and transparency toward us. If only they could have expressed the same affection *toward each other.*

The Mundane

Language at work was a problem, at least in the early days. The seconded officials, like Botha, were typically Afrikaners, and the language spoken at all meetings was Afrikaans. The meetings were held in Afrikaans even if some of the attendees' first language was Setswana or English, the latter being the case for consultants from Johannesburg. All South Africans were fluent in Afrikaans.

October 5

Another day of impressions so hard to record. Traveled from Tweespruit to the dam at Groethoek then to Thaba 'Nchu then the long drive to Taung.

Had a site meeting at Groethoek, felt I made a good impression, enjoyed meeting the RSA [South African] Water Commission people. Head of planning (design), an Englishman, had spent some time in Nashville, TN—small world.

So much in Afrikaans today, very important I pick it up.

October 13

Still not sure what I'm supposed to be doing at work, what my responsibilities are. Have good relationship with Botha, rather like working with him, despite his abrasiveness and frequent and loud confrontations with people (fortunately not with me yet!). Everything almost is in Afrikaans which makes me feel left out, sorta feel dumb. I know, too, that I am missing out on a lot I need to know.

Attending meetings held in a foreign language became tedious. I did not feel like I could participate, or even interrupt to ask questions comfortably, without prompting someone to wonder, *Why is this useless American here?* And that caused me to wonder, *Why IS this useless American here?* In the first few months, I was not productive.

October 30

The afternoon dragged by, did endless mundane tasks, spent a lot of time at the xerox machine—really wondered what am I doing here.

My work seemed mundane, but the travel and meetings opened many opportunities to talk about Jesus with businessmen. I was still learning to trust God with this way-of-life type of evangelism. I recorded two such experiences in my journal:

> *Botha wanted to have a "Bible chat" for the last 30 min. of work today with Alex, Mike & me. It got pretty good, went thru most of the steps to become a Jesus follower. Sometimes I have such a lack of vision for what God can and will do …*

> *Had a long political talk with a vendor representative named Thomas at his company office today. Managed to discuss spiritual things toward the end but I'm afraid I "bruised the fruit." I must always remember to value relationships, truly loving, over mere persuasion or (worse) argument.*

I relearned an essential lesson in the conversation with Thomas: the Bible says that without love, our words come across as a clanging gong.

Mankwe

In November, a new face entered the picture at the Department of Works: a Mr. de Wet. Almost immediately, he and Pretorius began talking to me about organizing a "national central workshop" for heavy equipment. The idea was to make use of an existing workshop at a remote location several hours from Mafikeng called *Mankwe* (MON quay).

This idea would require me to move to Mankwe. Team Leader John said that Crusade did not want me to move without a team of other Agape staff, and Crusade would not invest a team in Mankwe unless it was strategic from a ministry point of view. So, John sent my fellow engineer Alex and me on a field trip to Mankwe to reconnoiter.

We spent three hours on paved and unpaved roads and finally arrived at Mankwe. We found the large shop building and several supporting structures. But we did not find a town or village in the vicinity; very few people lived nearby. For Crusade, this location offered little in ministry potential. We also questioned whether this was a good location for a central workshop. A lowbed tractor-trailer hauling a piece of heavy equipment would have a four-to-five-hour haul from Mafikeng, and a six-to-eight-hour haul from Thaba 'Nchu.

We arrived at our conclusion in about fifteen minutes (Alex took some of our extra time to talk with the security guard about Jesus). There would be no move.

It was a flattering proposal, and I was anxious for a defined task. But God had not yet built the character and maturity in me that I would need for such a role—not to mention I lacked supervisory experience, workshop knowledge, and language skills. Crusade's requirement to keep our team together saved me, and the government, from failure.

From Mankwe, Alex and I took the opportunity to visit a hospital in the region. The facility was originally a mission hospital and, therefore, it was very old. The hospital was designed for 105 patients, but 200 beds were crammed into the facility.

The doctor was delighted to see us. I don't think he received many visitors, and he showed us around. I noted that the hospital's electrical generators were junk. Fortunately, a power line had recently been run to the facility, thereby connecting it to the power distribution grid. This brought to mind an account I had run across in the departmental files concerning a similar hospital that was not connected to the electrical grid.

The hospital in the file was provided electrical power by a diesel generator. The report to the departmental head office recounted the situation when the generator "packed up," meaning it quit working, and had to be sent to Johannesburg for repairs. Meanwhile, a backup generator took over, but it ran for only an hour before it also failed. The hospital then had no lights, but worse, no power for the electric water pumps. The hospital had a twelve-hour storage tank, but it ran dry. As a last resort, a diesel-engine-powered water pump was started, but it took ten minutes to fill a bucket.

The situation was desperate: imagine a hospital with minimal ability to wash wounds, hydrate patients, prepare meals, or flush toilets. It was unclear how long the facility operated under these constraints—at least a couple of days. Finally, a rented generator was trucked in from Johannesburg and power was restored until the original equipment could be returned. The report may have been trying to justify the rental cost.

These situations were so frustrating, because the potential for problems was so easy to foresee, but so little could be done, because so many facilities were in precisely the same predicament.

Chapter 9

THE FELLOWSHIP

The Bophu government had an unwritten policy that government workers should employ a domestic servant. The logic was that government employees were relatively well off and should help the unemployed. We never saw a formal mandate, but it was made clear through various channels that employing domestic help was a non-negotiable expectation.

When Joe, Mike, and I moved into our government house, we hired Dorcas as our housekeeper. Some friends of the ministry had recommended Dorcas, and she was indeed a good worker. She came faithfully, on time, two days a week to wash our clothes and clean our house. She renamed us "Joey, Marks, and Bully," and we learned to respond promptly when our names were called.

Dorcas wore a traditional long black dress and head wrap, so we had no idea if she was gray-haired. It was impossible to tell her age apart from her wrinkles, which indicated she was old.

She was respectful (sort of) because we were her employers but otherwise had no apprehension of any authority owed to us because we were Americans, or Jesus followers, or any trait we could muster up. Further, as bachelors, we started at a deficit respect-wise. Why had we not earned the cattle to pay *lobola*, the bride price? Shameful.

Communication could be tricky with Dorcas. She knew enough English to get a thought across, albeit with gesturing and occasional reversion to Afrikaans, which she seemed to favor over English. The most curious aspect of her English was her indiscriminate use of pronouns. To refer to an object, Dorcas might use it, him, her, he, she, or whatever else was mentally near at hand.

On her first day, Dorcas asked for two rand to buy a washboard in Mafikeng. When she came the next day, I expected the wood and metal scrub board, used before electric washers, that we see in museums of country life. But what she bought with the two rand was a piece of lumber, something like a finished shelf board, a bit over a half-meter long (about twenty inches). This Dorcas used as a scrub board in our bathtub to clean all of our clothes. She washed the clothes and hung them to dry on our circular clothesline in the backyard one day. The following day, she ironed the clothes. Dorcas ironed everything: shirts, shorts, underwear, pants, handkerchiefs, and socks. I don't remember her ironing towels and sheets, but every other fabric in the house felt the press of hot metal.

The clothes came out looking great; no laundry service could have done as well. They were all neatly stacked on our beds when we came in at night. Shirts were folded with buttons fastened down the front in a manner that I mimic today when folding a dress shirt. But it was a hard life for the clothing: over the course of two years, my underwear took on a see-through quality resembling mosquito netting.

Dorcas's observations on our behavior and complaints about our bachelor housekeeping could be sharp. Somehow, we ended up taking care of a cat for a few days. The cat did not like our bachelor ways either and proceeded to refine its new home by making deposits in the corners of our living room. Our floors were all linoleum, easier to clean than rugs, but Dorcas was livid anyway, and we got a verbal head-thumping over that boo-boo. She even had a relative write a letter to us to put her displeasure in clear, impossible-to-miss English to be absolutely sure we understood. *No animals in the house.* Check.

A side note: For the Tswana, pets do not receive a name like a person. That would be insulting to whoever might have that name. Animals are kept primarily for the utilitarian service they provide, such as dogs to guard the house or cats for killing snakes.

I was walking around the house barefoot one day and showed Dorcas my left foot with its missing two toes lost to my teenage lawn-mower accident. Her response was absent surprise or sympathy: "*Auk*, white children so naughty, all day run from house." So, it appeared she had previous experience working as a nanny. And it went without question that childhood injuries were due to the disobedience of the child. Dorcas cut no slack.

Dorcas took great pride in the appearance of our house. As she once said, a clean house was to "shine like a nail." We had a front porch, otherwise known as a "stoop," consisting of a concrete slab about two meters by three meters (six feet by nine feet). It was customary for stoops to be painted black, but mere paint was not socially acceptable. Every week, Dorcas cleaned away the ever-present dust, which could gather like miniature snowdrifts, and polished our stoop, with what I know not, so it shined "like a nail." It was so perfectly lustrous in the sunlight that we used the back door so as not to mess it up.

Our weekly association with Dorcas revealed another facet of the Tswana people. We could not have completely understood the Tswana's character—their pride, loyalty, and unstinting work ethic—without having Dorcas take care of us.

Church

Crusade had a well-developed plan—honed in many different countries—for starting a ministry in a new location like Bophu. The strategies were, first, a way-of-life outreach to people met in daily life contacts, such as neighbors or at work, and, second, assisting local churches in their ministry through training and a city-wide momentum event.

We built relationships in local churches as we had done during AIT in San Bernardino. Joe, Bonnie, and I began attending the Dutch Reformed Mission Church. Other team members attended the Methodist, Assembly of God, and Congregational churches.

The Dutch Reformed Church came to South Africa in 1652, when the Dutch East India Company established a re-supply station at Cape Town. The Dutch Reformed Church of the 1600s was rigorously Calvinistic in theology, meticulous in its application of the Bible, and austere in its practice. In the early days, women were obliged to wear full-length, high-necked "Mother Hubbard" dresses and men wore full beards with no mustache.

For its first two hundred years, the South African Dutch Reformed Church did not evangelize the black population. But this changed dramatically in 1860, when a fervent revival swept the Dutch churches in the colony around Cape Town. The revival produced so many conversions that churches knocked out walls to accommodate all the new Jesus followers. The revival was championed by Andrew Murray, the Afrikaans-speaking son of a Scottish missionary.

With the revival, the Dutch Reformed Church began evangelistic work with the black tribes as well as with people of mixed race, known in South Africa as "Coloured." The black Dutch Reformed *Mission* Church was established to serve black Africans. From inception, its congregations met separately from the white church's congregations.

Worship services at the Dutch Reformed Mission Church in Montshiwa were formal with a well-defined order of worship: hymns, a responsive reading, prayer, and a sermon. The clergy wore long black robes and spoke from an elevated pulpit, and the worshippers came in their best clothes. As a card-carrying Presbyterian, I felt right at home.

The hymns were all familiar ones that we sang in our churches in the States. The congregation stood, and a female voice called out the song number. When she began singing, the entire congregation joined in. Though we could only comprehend a few of the Setswana words, we could pronounce the words in the hymnal phonetically and thereby worship in song. The congregation intuitively sang harmony parts, and sometimes the men and women alternated singing lines to answer each other. The sweet lilting voices of the women contrasted with the low booming voices of the men. There were no instruments: it was all a cappella, and it was beautiful.

The sermons, however, took endurance, as we understood little. In one service, a layman delivered a forceful sermon in a voice that bordered on screaming. Joe commented afterward that he was prepared to use his CPR training because he thought the speaker was going to have a heart attack. We didn't know the topic, but Bonnie recognized the word *tsoga*, meaning wake up, used repeatedly. Using that word was ironic as it would have been impossible to sleep through the shattering oration.

The behavior of children during the service was extraordinary by Western standards. Babies were with their mothers, but crying was not a problem. Children up to adolescent age sat together in the first few rows of the hard wooden pews. The row of heads might bob around, but the children were absolutely quiet throughout the entire service. If a child made so much as a peep, any adult was authorized to deliver a sharp knuckle rap on the crown of the close-cropped little head.

The churches in Montshiwa and Mafikeng were approached at one time or another about their interest in Crusade's ministry. We talked to the pastor of the Dutch Reformed Mission Church several times.

The Good and the Ugly

A close team is particularly important when living overseas with its cultural pressures. You need someone to validate that, even though you are different from the surrounding culture, you are normal. (That is, normal for one crazy enough to move overseas!)

Our team leaders, John and Lynn, focused on building team unity through retreats, prayer times, and weekly team meetings in which we shared a meal, had devotions, discussed the ministry, and received a scripture lesson or training. At one point, we took a college-level course on the book of John as a group.

We combined into sub-groups for projects and outreaches. For example, we tag-teamed the teaching role in conferences or seminars, and we co-led Bible studies. In addition to ministry, we occasionally found ourselves working together in our vocational assignments.

We spent all our off-time together too: going to a nearby drive-in movie, viewing slide shows from our holiday trips, playing hyper-competitive Risk games, and jogging together. We occasionally had access to tennis courts and a run-down, questionably-healthy swimming pool (the water was a dark indeterminate color). We passed around the *Time* magazine from home and had long talks about how to solve President Jimmy Carter's problems.

With time, I was comfortable in work, ministry, or play with any combination of my teammates. I doubt any of us could have survived, or grown as we did, if we had been alone.

However, before we get too far into "rainbows and unicorns" country, it's important to reveal we had a troublemaker.

We took turns driving to work at the Imperial Reserve, which was five minutes away, maybe fifteen if we got behind a donkey cart. We could easily go home for lunch at our 12:45 p.m. break.

At lunch it looked at first as though I'd been left behind and I really reacted bad to that, but then Mike came & got me and we went to eat at John & Lynn's. While there, Mike brought up the point that we should be back at work at 1:45 instead of 2:00. Boy did I react poor to that ...

God is working in my life but it's painful sometimes. How my life reeks of self ...

My behavior was painful for my conscience, and I'm sure it was painful for those around me too. I could be short-tempered and easily offended, like I was with the car-buying decision. I recorded in my journal:

Joe seems set on a sedan; Mike goes along but I know he feels we should get a van for the sake of the team. I've gotten so jealous and snippy, "I have my rights," that I don't know what I want.

Reacting negatively to others could also come out at work. A journal entry recorded that I became "fed up" with Botha and told him so. I noted that my reaction was "not walking in the Spirit," so at least my conscience was engaged. (Even if my sense of self protection was not; Botha was twice my size.)

Lynn once told me, "When God gets through with you, you'll be so beautiful." Her comment was a tactful way of saying that God had a whole lot to do because I could be *ugly*. I knew Crusade was made up of imperfect people when I joined, but it was a shock to realize that I was imperfect too. Suffice it to say (for now), my teammates unknowingly, purely by the gracious way they responded to me, urged me on from ugliness to internal beauty.

> *I'm constantly reminded of the verse "to whom much is given much is required." Surely, we have been given much, materially and in each other as a team.*

Chapter 10

THE HIKE

December of 1978 was our first Christmas away from home, and we needed team fellowship as the "ointment" for the absence of family. We drew names and hand-crafted Christmas gifts for each other. I made a bulletin board for Cindy. Joe made a desk for me.

December was also the month of the annual southern Africa staff conference. Every year, all of the Crusade staff members throughout southern Africa, some one hundred strong, gathered for training, fellowship, and updates on the worldwide ministry. In 1978, the ten-day conference was held at the campus of the new University of Durban-Westville in the modern city of Durban, the largest port in Africa.

All that we had seen of South Africa so far was windy grassland, the dusty township of Montshiwa, and the shops of small-town Mafikeng. We took the kombi and two other cars and headed to Johannesburg to spend the night.

The next day, we merged onto the South African equivalent of a four-lane American interstate and headed southeast for the all-day drive to Durban. About midway, the jagged peaks of the Drakensberg Mountains, like the spine of a dragon, rose out of the grassland. It was much like driving west on I-70 across the plains of eastern Colorado and watching the Rockies rise out of the western horizon. We weaved through the mountains, then down into the lush hills of the Natal province, as we headed toward the sandy coast of the Indian Ocean.

The conference teaching and presentations were world-class, featuring speakers from all over Africa and flown in from the US. Rubbing shoulders with staff from other countries in southern Africa was enlightening and encouraging.

Staff from each country presented reports. Most memorable was the report about the large numbers of Rhodesians who were becoming Jesus followers in the midst of war. Rhodesia, now Zimbabwe, was a former British colony on the northern border of South Africa.

We absorbed rich teaching from the Bible. One talk outlined how South Africa was violating God's moral law: "Do to others as you would have them do to you" (Luke 6:31).

In the prayer room, we each picked a time and prayed for an African country. Following typical Crusade practice, a day of witnessing was on the agenda; Steve and I talked with a retired fellow on the beach about Jesus.

December 15 (Durban)

Another fulfilling day of staff training. My life since joining staff has been so much richer ...

The conference agenda also included time for fellowship, team sports, and even a talent show. One staffer played the violin, another the trombone. A choral group of black and white Africans sang praise songs. One national team went so far as to work up a comedy skit—that was us. I have a tape recording of our practice session in Montshiwa, and we could hardly finish practicing the skit for laughing. In our humble opinion, it would knock 'em dead. Which was true, sorta.

Our skit was a lampoon of a tent revival, with one of my teammates acting as a firebrand preacher. It started auspiciously like this: "What do you get if you take the 'd' off devil, you get evil, and that's what you'll be if you follow the devil, you'll be evil!"

The sermon proceeded with an exegesis of each letter in the word devil:

> take the "e" from evil and you have "vil" and the devil will make you vile,

take the "v" from vil and you have "il" and the devil will make you ill,

take the "i" from il and you have "l," "and hell is where you go if you follow the devil!"

Having rescued our listeners from "l," we ran out of letters and, mercifully, sermon material. After the sermon, the team sang as a choir to invite the audience to "turn now or burn, repent you worm ..." You get the drift.

We awaited the thunderous ovation, but it turned out we had a tough crowd. We heard scattered laughter and clapping, saw crossed arms and shaking heads, and also observed a few puzzled faces wondering if they had boarded this conference in error. Some of our fellow staffers enjoyed the pun, but some considered it poor taste, or didn't "get it." One American remarked, "This can be a lesson for all of us." Oh boy.

The murmuring was a shocker, but it should not have been. After all, our audience included black South Africans of various tribes and languages, white South Africans both Afrikaans- and English-speaking, multiracial groups from other countries, and finally, Americans from all across the varied regions of the US. And this diversity was overlaid with assorted church denominations. Social time with this menagerie of nationalities and ethnicities was like cultural hopscotch.

But of course, when we explained the innocent intention of the joke, our brothers and sisters proved they were such by giving us hugs, belated laughter, and full acceptance. If we were to make a cultural mistake, this was where to do it: surrounded by agape love.

This conference, held during apartheid, could be a model of how to deal with cultural and racial interaction among Jesus followers. Having a common sovereign—Jesus—and following his command to love one another prevents so many problems. Or the love of Jesus cures problems, such as with our culture-confusing skit.

As the conference ended, we left encouraged. The conference had been horizon-stretching and heart-inspiring.

December 17 (Durban)

My big consolation as I wonder about my life is that I know that right now I'm where God wants me, doing what He wants me to do and that His purposes for leading me here are of eternal and infinite value. That's comforting.

Christmas

After the conference, the singles spent some vacation time camping out. We took the kombi and Steve and Duane's Ford and headed for the Royal Natal National Park in the Drakensberg Mountains.

December 26 (Just outside Royal Natal Nat'l Park)

We spent last Thursday shopping in Durban ("we" being the Bophu singles), had to fight the urge to buy the store out at Hyper Market [like a Wal-Mart]. Friday we left for the mountains ...

December in the Southern Hemisphere is mid-summer and mid-holidays, and the park was full of South Africans in their travel trailers, so we camped on an adjacent farmer's property. The farmer earned side revenue from the park overflow; he even provided showers with water heated by a wood-fired stove.

We pitched our two tents—a pup tent for the girls (sorry) and a huge tent the guys had borrowed from Mr. Botha. We set up on a grassy *koppie* (CAW pea), a small hill, overlooking a long verdant valley and a stone-filled mountain stream, with a spectacular view of the "Amphitheatre." This feature was a half-moon of flat-topped mountains with a white waterfall, in miniature because of the distance, cascading down one side. It was picture-postcard beautiful.

Except for the rain.

Sat, Sun, Mon it rained. We did some basket buying from some kids on the roadside Sunday.

The basket buying left a mark. The boys were local black children, maybe eight to ten years old, barefoot, and dressed in the typical ragged shirts and shorts. I found myself haggling with one of them over a certain basket; he wanted one rand and I wanted to give him eighty cents. Somewhere during this high-stakes negotiation, the Holy Spirit seemed to speak to me, saying, *What are you doing?* I immediately gave the boy the one rand. If I had thought harder about it, I would have given him ten. Why was a comparative millionaire arguing over twenty cents with a poor country boy? Jesus would never have done that. It's a lesson that has stuck: generosity should be proportional to your means.

When December 25 dawned, we were all homesick. We didn't have the trappings of the day—tree, lights, and home-cooked holiday feasts—but more importantly, we had no contact with our families. However, we had each other.

But if team fellowship was the ointment for homesickness, it was about to get a fly in it. We decided to take a hike when the rain stopped on Christmas Day. My December 26 journal entry chronicled the excursion:

> *About noon we set out on a major trek to the "gorge," a certain spot in the "Amphitheatre." The terrain was beautiful. In some of the "hollows" there was lush growth which reminded me of the Smokies.*

Along the way were springbok, a deer that is the emblem for South Africa, and baboons. It felt exotic, although these sightings were equivalent to seeing common wildlife in the Smoky Mountains back in Tennessee.

> *The day wore on and we finally got to a narrow canyon we guessed was the gorge. We pushed on and made a poor decision to ford two streams to get to this chain ladder deal that went up the bluffs into the overgrown hillside. After another 30 minutes of thrashing around we gave up on finding a climax to our trip and went back down. By now we were under pressure to hustle because the gate to the park closed at sundown (8 we thought, was really 7). Now we began to get a little frayed, everyone tired and a long way to go.*

> *Getting dark and the trail was hard to follow. Somewhere we ended up on an old trail that was washed out in places. It was a real stress time ... Everybody had their own opinion, teamwork was not real good.*

We survived but were physically and emotionally drained. Feelings were bruised but would heal; there had been good intentions, if not good sense, all around. The five guys were chivalrously concerned with the safety of the two single gals the whole time. We learned that we needed cool heads and a servant's heart when under stress.

The next day a new problem developed: About twenty-four hours after the hike, Ann suddenly bolted for the farmer's fence, leaned over the top strand of barbed wire, and upended her stomach. Her condition went downhill, literally, as the day wore on with more gastric problems. Ann wanted to go to the hospital, and later she wanted to fly home to Wisconsin! By the following day, Ann felt better, and we struck out for Montshiwa in the hope of getting her to our friend Dr. Ben at Bophelong hospital.

No good. Ann got worse, and we decided we would have to trust a South African doctor. We stopped in a small town called Ficksburg and got her in to see a physician. He measured Ann's temperature, and it was 104 degrees. The good doctor turned out to be a Christian, and he and his equally good wife insisted all five of us stay in their home. The hospitality of South Africans of either race was truly overwhelming. We compromised and the guys rented hotel rooms so as not to impose too much of a burden. The next day, the doctor put Ann in the local hospital to treat her for dehydration.

With Ann safely recovering in the hospital, we took a side trip to the nearby tiny country of Lesotho. Lesotho is a geopolitical oddity: it's completely surrounded by South Africa but independent (truly independent). Raising sheep is a major part of the Lesotho economy, and we bought woolen tapestries at a roadside market run by some expatriate Americans who strangely had absolutely no interest in talking with other Americans. They were so turned off to us, I wondered if they had murdered someone or robbed a bank back home, à la *Butch Cassidy and the Sundance Kid*.

On Saturday, Ann was weak but stable. We checked her out of the hospital, headed north, and by six that evening we pulled into Montshiwa. Ann stayed at our North American oasis, Ben and Cathy's house, to recover.

The same bug eventually went through all of us. For me, it morphed into a cross-cultural rejection.

January 7 (Montshiwa)

After the trip to Ficksburg we all came down with gastro illnesses with symptoms like diarrhea, nausea, cramps, headaches.

Everything seems to literally make me sick, besides food, our house, my room, the pelt on my wall, even my attitudes toward people, the different way of life in S.A., single star hotels. The thought of these and myriad more turns my stomach.

I'd been praying that God would wake me up and turn me to Himself. He's being faithful; all else is revolting.

So ended our first Christmas. The experiences of our first three months—settling in, starting work and ministry, the staff conference, travel, and illness—were a forge in which the Lord welded us together into a team.

1979

"You would not have called to me unless I had been calling to you," said the Lion.
—C. S. Lewis, *The Silver Chair*

Thurs, Oct. 6, 1978

Dear Family,

This has been an exciting week as we began work this week. We engineers went to the Dept. of Works Monday and almost immediately lined up to be useful...

Chapter 11

THE LIFELINE

Culture stress arises from the many daily transactions needed to live life. In a foreign culture, these simple but necessary tasks become harder to complete, leading to an underlying tension or anxiety. In the first few months, we did nothing on autopilot; every interaction with the culture took extra thought and energy. We often had our guards up and we felt misunderstood much of the time.

Let's start with that most fundamental freedom in the US: driving a car.
- South Africans, as a former British colony, drive on the left side of the road. When making a turn—left turns in particular—one can end up on the wrong side facing oncoming traffic.
- Then there were the roundabouts—a fiendish invention that in heavy traffic traps the novice in an infinite carousel of cars. For some time, driving was scary …
- … and embarrassing. I'm sure some Africans noted the silly Americans getting into our vehicle, shutting the door, and only then realizing the steering wheel was in front of the other seat.
- To drive legally, it took days at the regional magistrate's office to obtain a Bophu license. Many times I used the expression, "No, I can't come back next week."

Dealing with inexperienced bureaucracy for mundane yet vital tasks could be tedious. For example, when mailing one of many international packages at our small post office, I was once served by a new postal clerk. The ensuing negotiation went something like this:

"*Dumela ma*, hello miss. I want to send this package to Alabama in the United States."

The postal clerk weighs the package and references a well-worn paperback rate book, then looks up with a tentative suggestion and says, "Ten rand thirty."

"It was less the last time, are you sure?" the American patron counters.

More reference to said rate book; consultation in Setswana with a colleague who responds with an *auk* and a shrug. Another gambit is offered: "Eight rand forty."

"I don't think that's the right amount," I reply.

Some head scratching.

I make a counteroffer, saying, "Would seven rand fifty be enough?"

Sold! The clerk accepts the counteroffer. Then an ink-filled potato masher is used to stamp the package energetically and repeatedly (well, you gotta be sure 'cause it's going a long way). I watch with trepidation as the officially defaced parcel disappears into the bowels of the post office for its journey halfway around the planet.

Culture stress situations included cringing at a tighter norm for personal space, wondering if the price offered was good or a gouge, urgently fumbling for the word for "restroom," asking why things were so messy or rules so rigid, complaining about multiple languages (two of which seem redundant), wondering why that person laughed or shouted at me, and asking repeatedly why must the wind blow all of the time.

Another innocent African practice that was stressful, at least at first, was related to friendly greetings between guys. We would meet a Tswana friend on the street who was happy to see us and, sometimes, he might want to hold hands with us for a few minutes—that is, left hand clasping the right hand. This was a sign of sincere appreciation, even admiration, without any of the Western cultural connotations. It was equivalent to shaking hands, but for an American guy, it was awkward. It was as uncomfortable to us as the practice in some European countries of male friends greeting each other with a kiss on the cheek.

Studies of the phenomena of culture stress, alternatively referred to as culture shock, say that a person immersed in a foreign culture for an extended time goes through several phases of emotion. The first phase is exhilaration: *Wow, everything is different and exciting!* Conquering bits of the language is a delight; learning to read a map or a train schedule are fun triumphs. Most tourists never leave this phase and go home with rose-colored euphoria over their travels.

The excitement may last a month or more and is followed by a month or more of feeling that the culture is different and strange. The culture begins to seem more peculiar than exciting. After initial success, language learning becomes difficult.

Then, at the bottom of the curve, is when the culture begins to feel ridiculous. The emotion at this point is frustration and disdain. One may distrust the native population, emotional and even physical fatigue sets in, and work productivity typically sags.

The next phase in cultural adaptation is acceptance. I call it the "Sigh Plateau," in which a sigh of, *Oh yeah, I remember how this works,* replaces frustration. The expatriate learns the ropes and can anticipate and be patient with the differences.

Attaining the Sigh Plateau is expedited by recognizing that the service providers often see the expatriate's requests as at best non-routine, and more likely as weird. The needs of the impatient foreigner are probably outside their job description. That creates stress and extra work on their side of the counter.

For example, somewhere in our preparation to go to South Africa, we were told it was customary to ask for a 10 percent discount when paying in cash. So, in our first few months, we asked shop owners for 10 percent off the cost of our transactions. Along the way, we dropped this practice after observing that most transactions were in cash and nobody else seemed to be asking for discounts. We had been misinformed: asking for a discount for payment in cash was NOT customary. Retail buying and selling worked the same way as in the US. And yet the small-town Mafikeng stores dutifully complied with our request and discounted our purchases, probably thinking this was customary in America.

I cringe to think of the image we presented those first few months. I wonder if the shopkeepers, when they saw us coming, cried out, "*Auk nie,* the American scrooges are back!"

As the New Year dawned, we were gradually crossing into the cultural acceptance phase. We adapted to lifestyle differences and learned new ways to communicate, enabling us to be more at ease. There were ongoing cultural surprises, but we coped better.

For instance, we found that our lifeline home—the mail service—was reliable, and the cost was dependable, once both sides of the counter learned how the rate book worked. Remarkably, very few of our hundreds of mailed items were damaged or lost in the two years we spent in Bophu. I once mailed a collection of southern African currency home in a plain envelope. It arrived in Alabama with no problem.

We adapted to the culture of Bophu relatively quickly. We were blessed to serve in a country with religious freedom, where our native language was widely spoken, and where clean water and food were readily available. Also, we had experienced friends like Ben and Cathy to help us cope. Without these advantages, it would be a longer, steeper climb to the Sigh Plateau.

Mail

I don't know how I would have kept my sanity—such as it was—living overseas for so long without hearing from home. About the time that the longing for something familiar and the drag of being a foreigner would gang up to pull me down, a letter or parcel would arrive and spark a flicker of excitement. It was impossible not to smile when opening mail from home. Mail reminded me that there were those like me who loved me, and there were those like me who believed in what I was doing.

Dependence on snail mail may seem strange with today's instantaneous communication, but we checked our post office boxes every day. Sometimes twice.

My mother made it her mission to keep the postal stream flowing. A quick count of the surviving letters from home works out to more than one a week, not counting packages. Dad enjoyed making cassette tape recordings. (He hosted a show on the Roanoke radio station with the moniker "Uncle Jay.") In addition to personal messages, Dad recorded football games, newscasts, a family reunion, Thanksgiving dinner, a barbershop quartet, and a Billy Graham crusade.

It turned out to be crucial to pay extra to specify *par avion*, air-mail service, for letters and packages sent either to or from the US. My mom sent a round tin of brownies by surface mail and the package took two months to arrive. Compounding the delay, the package went to the country of *Botswana* before it was redirected to *Bophuthatswana*. When I finally received it, the brownies were compacted into a six-inch disk from rolling around in the hold of a ship. The compressed confections resembled an oversize hockey puck except that they were green from mold all over and all the way through. Not a crumb was edible; in a letter to Mom I noted, "We all cried."

In addition to mail from my immediate family, I received letters from friends and extended family who asked about me and assured me they were praying for me. This was so encouraging. My pastor, Frank Barker, used his valuable time to write several letters.

Two of my friends from Birmingham, a guy and a gal, had been writing to me independently for a few months. Then, they individually told me they had started dating. After that, the letters included their parallel views of how the relationship was developing. After about six months, they both wrote, separately, to say they were engaged. Later in the year they married, yet they still wrote, now as a couple. As time passed, they wrote about buying a house and having a baby. It was fun and refreshing to follow their lives. I eventually returned the series of letters to them as a family keepsake.

My goal was to mail something to my family every Thursday, be it a letter (or aerogram), card, cassette tape, or package. I didn't miss many weeks because I didn't want Mom to worry.

Part of our Crusade job description was to regularly post printed "prayer letters" to friends and supporters with updates on the ministry and our lives in general. I supplemented the prayer letters with personal notes—from time to time I sent individual letters to every financial and prayer supporter.

A significant part of my spare time went into writing correspondence. And a significant part of this messenger's comfort and courage came enclosed in the letters that I received.

The Lifeline

It turned out to be crucial to pay extra to specify *par avion,* air-mail service, for letters and packages sent either to or from the US. My mom sent a round tin of brownies by surface mail and the package took two months to arrive. Compounding the delay, the package went to the country of *Botswana* before it was redirected to *Bophuthatswana*. When I finally received it, the brownies were compacted into a six-inch disk from rolling around in the hold of a ship. The compressed confections resembled an oversize hockey puck except that they were green from mold all over and all the way through. Not a crumb was edible; in a letter to Mom I noted, "We all cried."

In addition to mail from my immediate family, I received letters from friends and extended family who asked about me and assured me they were praying for me. This was so encouraging. My pastor, Frank Barker, used his valuable time to write several letters.

Two of my friends from Birmingham, a guy and a gal, had been writing to me independently for a few months. Then, they individually told me they had started dating. After that, the letters included their parallel views of how the relationship was developing. After about six months, they both wrote, separately, to say they were engaged. Later in the year they married, yet they still wrote, now as a couple. As time passed, they wrote about buying a house and having a baby. It was fun and refreshing to follow their lives. I eventually returned the series of letters to them as a family keepsake.

My goal was to mail something to my family every Thursday, be it a letter (or aerogram), card, cassette tape, or package. I didn't miss many weeks because I didn't want Mom to worry.

Part of our Crusade job description was to regularly post printed "prayer letters" to friends and supporters with updates on the ministry and our lives in general. I supplemented the prayer letters with personal notes—from time to time I sent individual letters to every financial and prayer supporter.

A significant part of my spare time went into writing correspondence. And a significant part of this messenger's comfort and courage came enclosed in the letters that I received.

Chapter 12

THE MOSAIC

The New Year dawned on a Monday, which fortunately was a holiday since we were still feeling woozy from our camping sickness. For me, the only thing that tasted good was Coca-Cola, the one American product that was the same as at home.

Returning to work we learned a nice South African New Year's custom, which I noted in a journal entry.

> *It is appropriate to give a person a personal handshake and a special greeting, wish for the New Year, etc., the first time you see them after the 1st of the year.*

On Tuesday, January 2, I was back at my seat in a corner of Mr. Botha's office when Mr. de Wet came in. At first, he talked about the now-defunct idea of a central workshop in Mankwe. Then, with no warning, he said, "Ready to come to my section?" Botha was seated at his desk glaring and steaming, but he said nothing. Apparently, this move had already been discussed and approved with departmental management.

I followed my new supervisor down the courtyard sidewalk to his office. Mr. de Wet's section was responsible for mechanical equipment, and he casually mentioned I would be reorganizing the section. His nonchalance gave no hint of the new tracks this assignment put under my calling.

Mr. de Wet scooted a clerk out of her desk to give it to me and made an announcement to his staff, which was something like, "*Bull* Norton is from the US, from a university, and you are to go to Mr. Norton with any equipment questions." Shazam—just like that, I was deemed the man with equipment omniscience, the "dozer whisperer," if you will.

I was now responsible for arguably the most overlooked mess in the Bophu government, which was saying a lot given the number of messes spread liberally around the homeland. My assigned mess was a fleet of hundreds (who knew how many) of expensive, yet neglected, construction, road, and stationary equipment spread over hundreds of kilometers (who knew how far) of half-forgotten back country. The government's equipment fleet had large financial and public service impacts, yet was all but ignored and had been, seemingly, for years.

I was up for the challenge. In my former role, I had been tagging behind Mr. Botha in endless meetings all in Afrikaans. Others found Botha difficult, but he and I got along fine (well, most of the time). We could even joke around; he called me "*Bully* the kid." I liked working for this type of person because he was transparent. However, my inability to contribute in my role with him was frustrating.

In the new role, I could use my engineering skills, and the task of reorganizing the area was motivating. As I had with Botha, I traveled frequently with Mr. de Wet.

January 11 (Thaba 'Nchu)

On my first overnight trek with my new boss Mr. de Wet. His style is more like mine, and he's very gung ho.

America is fairly termed a "melting pot," but South Africa is more like a mosaic. I found this in the names of the towns we passed through on my job-related treks:

Vergenoug (FUR he knock), named for the point where a wagon train of Afrikaner settlers, known as boers (boors), meaning farmer in Dutch, decided they had traveled "far enough" inland.

Thaba 'Nchu, the "black mountain," where an isolated band of Tswana fought off Zulu marauders while the rest of the tribe fled north.

Mafikeng, the "place of stones," where Robert Baden-Powell, a

British army officer, got the idea for the Boy Scouts during the British Empire's war with the Afrikaans republics (the "Boer War").

Hotazel (Ha TAZ el), named for a farm near the Kalahari Desert that was "hot as hades."

Stella, meaning "star," named for the appearance of a comet and once the capital of the short-lived Republic of Stellaland.

Kuruman (COO ruh mun), the site of the first London Missionary Society station, founded by Robert Moffat in 1821. Moffat translated the Bible into Setswana, and his daughter married David Livingstone of Stanley and Livingstone fame ("Dr. Livingstone, I presume?").

South Africa arguably has more intriguing historical anomalies per square mile than anywhere else on the continent.

A Second Wife

In my new role, I supervised three file room clerks. They made life more interesting. A January journal entry recorded the discussion below.

> *I have three Tswana clerks who help me in my vocational position at the Department of Works. Two of them are women. Last week I entered their office right in the middle of a very spirited discussion the two women were having in their native tongue of Setswana. One of them explained to me in English that they were arguing over the advantage/disadvantage of a woman who was barren allowing her husband to take a second wife so that there would be children in the family (a high priority in African culture). They wanted my opinion.*
>
> *I explained carefully that God had instituted marriage and had set it up for one man & one woman. I explained that He loves us more than we can understand, and knows perfectly what's best for us. He will meet our needs whether it be with a marriage of children or one without. They did not seem overly impressed with my point ...*

The best way to answer a moral question from a different culture is to apply scripture. In my explanation of God's original marriage intent, a quote on marriage from Genesis or the New Testament would have been more effective. A Westerner speaking on cultural mores can be shrugged off, but the Bible transcends all cultures.

Domestic Matters

On the home front, Joe, Mike, and I had settled into a cooking and cleanup schedule. The kitchen in our new home came with an electric stove, a small refrigerator, and a Formica table. We added a metal pantry, dishes, and a toaster. We bought fabric and Ann made us curtains. If I do say so, except for the stack of spare kombi tires we stored in one corner, it was neat and tidy. My mom would have been proud; she had cried when she visited my college hovels. It was ironic that I lived better in Africa as a missionary than I did in America as a hippie.

Outside, we planted kikuyu grass and a couple of jacaranda trees in our front yard. In the back, we planted a grapefruit tree, but we left the ground unimproved. The neighborhood boys used our yard for soccer games and grass would never have survived; Joe and Mike joined them sometimes. The easy lending policy of Joe with his soccer ball was a kid magnet. On Sundays when we got home from church, the boys were waiting on our stoop to borrow the ball.

In February, the last three members of the Bophu team arrived from the States. Nancy, an occupational therapist, would work at Bophelong hospital, and a married couple, Ron and Bev, a pharmacist and nurse respectively, would live and work at a clinic about two hours away. Now the team was complete at fourteen members: eight singles and three married couples.

Nancy roomed with Ann and Bonnie in their government house located just up the dusty lane from Joe, Mike, and me. There were now three single gals to five single guys on the team. The odds were improving.

I won't blame Nancy's addition as the catalyst for the raid on our house. I'll simply observe that we had no problems with the "sorority" up the road until a therapist was living among them. We arrived home one evening to find the labels removed from the cans in our pantry, our socks mismatched, our beds short-sheeted, etc. I found the initials 'B-A-N' (Bonnie-Ann-Nancy) in multiple colors embroidered across the hindquarters of my long underwear. The team's single ladies needed more to do.

Soon after the intrusion, the five single guys graciously asked the single ladies over to our house for a nice, somewhat edible dinner. I think it was my mom's spaghetti recipe using the most familiar pasta we could find. Mike, Joe, and I bustled around our little house getting everything cleaned up and cooked up. It was the first of many group "dates." We even turned out the lights and used candles on the table.

About halfway through the entrée, we heard a knock on the front door. When it was opened, one of our neighbors entered without a word and walked to the hallway, opened the fuse box, and squinted at the fuses. He was an older Tswana, a government worker like us, with perfect English.

"Can we help you?" I inquired of our visitor.

"I'm trying to ascertain which fuse has gone out," replied our neighbor.

"Oh, haha, the fuses are fine."

"But your lights are off."

"Yes, we turned them off so we could use candles."

"Why would you use candles when you have electricity?"

"Uh, well you see, back home it's considered romantic to use candles."

"It's romantic in America to pretend you are poor?"

I'm sure this story spread through the neighborhood leading to much shaking of heads at our expense. No doubt mothers applied the Tswana version of "bless their hearts."

Lost in the Weeds

While our team life was fun, my work life kept being punctuated with unexpected new chapters.

It appears de Wet will become a regional manager and I will stay to work with the reorganization in Montshiwa.

In Alabama we have an expression for a turn of events such as this: "Say what?" (Spoken with a robust emphasis on "what" and a tone of exasperation, like when your mother calls dinner for the third time.)

It was a complete surprise that de Wet wanted to move from his role at the departmental headquarters and into a role in an outlying regional office. With his departure, I had no supervision. My job responsibilities had progressed from under-utilized, to over-committed, to lost-in-the-weeds.

My vocational role was convoluted, but what about my development of a personal ministry?

> *I had my first ministry appointment today but it was pretty much of a flop. I want to just give up with all the ministry business but I can't with the lessons God had taught me about walking by faith. He will bring fruit if I will continue to be faithful.*

I noted in my February journal that "nobody is panning out." These notes were references to my opening attempt at organizing a Bible study, or discipleship group, as we had been taught to do in AIT. My initial attempts at forming a small group felt uncomfortable. I was, after all, lightly experienced in ministry. This awkwardness combined with the difficulty in getting contacts to show up was discouraging.

So, both work and ministry were frustrating. Lest I have a pity party, maybe it was a good time for a lesson in humility.

Walking in His Shoes

We occasionally discarded old clothing or household items, but we did not need to look for a charity: Dorcas took all of our old belongings as if they were some sort of treasure. She even took my worn-out pair of brown men's shoes with the right sole flapping at the toe.

Over time, we learned that Dorcas had a son.

It was sometime later, on a Saturday morning, that a young Tswana man knocked on our front door. We opened the door, and the young man stepped in and immediately took a seat in one of our living room chairs. We sat down as well, smiled, and patiently waited. We had learned that this no-introduction-make-yourself-at-home behavior was a perfectly acceptable African entrance. The best thing to do was to take a seat and nod pleasantly, knowing an explanation would come with time, and then to prepare tea. The young man was dressed in a buttoned coat and a tie, which were old but obviously his best clothes. After some minutes the silence was broken.

"I am Dorcas's son, Joseph."

"Oh!" we exclaimed in unison, and then we exchanged greetings in Setswana, and English too, since it was obvious that Dorcas's son had a considerably better grasp of English than Dorcas. We proceeded to heat the teapot and explore conversation. He was in high school and hoped to matriculate (graduate) soon. We talked about soccer, church choirs, and other topics that were interesting to a Tswana youth of his age.

It was during Joseph's explanation to Joe of which soccer team was the best that I happened to look down at his feet. I noticed that he was wearing a well-worn pair of brown men's shoes with the right sole flapping at the toe.

I've heard it said that all Americans are rich in the eyes of the world because even our poorest live better than the vast majority of the world. I've also heard it said that an American that makes $35,000 per year is in the top 1 percent of the world population in terms of wealth. But cold statistics can never humble as much as meeting a young man in his best clothes who is proudly wearing the shoes you discarded as worn out.

On one occasion, we went to see where Dorcas lived. It was a traditional red mud house with a thatched roof in one of the outlying villages from Montshiwa.

She was excited to see us but embarrassed that she wasn't dressed well ... Seeing her place helped us understand a little better why she is sometimes so defensive & so prideful of our place. Makes me appreciate the way God has blessed us too.

Our concrete-block government house was humble by Western standards, but a few miles away, our hardworking housekeeper lived in the third world. And even Dorcas in her thatched-roof house with a mielie plot as a front yard was better off than the destitute in the shanty-filled *barrio* we had visited in Mexico and the squatter camps that existed in other parts of South Africa. I mused in my journal:

In the States, poverty was in pockets and not so untreatable. Here poverty is the norm and is so vast that it can only be dealt with in pockets ...

When one sees such poor standards of living, and if you know the character of the people living there, one can only conclude that we Americans have scarcely a hint, only a faint conception, of how richly God has blessed our land.

From Campus Crusade for Christ Bophutatswana Pictorial Edition of *Have You Heard of the Four Spiritual Laws?* © 1980 Campus Crusade for Christ, Inc. All rights reserved. Used with permission.

Chapter 13

THE BIRTH

Our basic unit of training for groups such as churches was called a LIFE seminar (the name is derived from "Lay Institute For Evangelism"). A LIFE seminar taught participants how to share their faith in Jesus as an everyday way of life. The first LIFE was scheduled for March and we printed a publicity brochure that read:

> The INTRODUCTORY COURSE will help you to:
> - Apply basic spiritual principles for consistently experiencing the abundant Christian life.
> - Share the Gospel through New Testament evangelism.
> - Overcome your fears and anxieties about sharing your faith.

We had secured a Montshiwa school building for the teaching portion of the seminar. The highlight was Saturday afternoon when we went door-to-door in the local neighborhood to talk with the residents about Jesus. Then we regrouped so the participants could share their "war stories," that is, experiences while sharing their faith in the community.

Two churches signed on to be a part of our first LIFE seminar and we had a substantial turnout of twenty-five attendees. Our prayer target had been larger, forty to sixty, but the number that came was just the right size for pairing between trainees and Crusade staff.

The government and community leaders that we had invited did not show. Likewise, it was disappointing that the larger churches did not sign up. In our weekly staff meeting, the team had been listening to a teaching in which Jesus tells the apostle Paul, "My power is made perfect in weakness" (2 Corinthians 12:9). The teaching, by a pastor named Ron Dunn, pointed out that God uses weak people, those without much power in the world's eyes.

The co-director of the Campus Crusade ministry for South Africa, Siphu Benghu, attended this seminar, our first, to give us moral support and encouragement. Siphu had been to the US and spoken at Briarwood. He was a good friend of Frank Barker; Briarwood was even part of his financial support team. We were delighted to meet each other.

The Birth Following Birth

On the second night, we broke up into twos or threes for practice. I paired up with Cyrus, the assistant principal at the technical school. We had already struck up a friendship by talking about the training of mechanics.

The content of a LIFE seminar revolved around the use of *The Four Spiritual Laws*. Cyrus and I sat next to each other to practice using the booklet. I went first and read to my partner as if he was hearing it for the first time. Cyrus listened intently and began to ask thoughtful questions. At first, I assumed his questions were role-play, that is, I thought he was trying to mimic how a person that did not know Jesus might respond. But it became clear the further we went into the booklet that Cyrus was asking the questions for real, and he was asking for himself.

We got to the question page that asks if the person wanted to make Jesus Christ Lord of their life. Cyrus asked, "I had to work and struggle to learn English. Isn't becoming a Christian like learning a language?"

"No," I answered, "becoming a Christian is like being born all over again." I went on to explain that it's not something you work for, and it's more than something you know in your mind. I told Cyrus that Jesus once told Nicodemus, a religious leader, that he needed a spiritual birth and with that rebirth he would receive a new spiritual life. "And you can be born again by asking Jesus to come into your life," I said.

"Then, yes, I'd like to receive Christ," Cyrus responded.

We stepped outside and Cyrus prayed, "Jesus, I know I have sinned; please forgive me. I want you to sit on the throne of my life. I open the door of my life for you. Please come into my life and make me the kind of person you want me to be."

With that prayer, Cyrus stepped from death to life. The words were different, but he prayed with a sincere heart, just as I had done four years before as a college student.

Then we went over assurance—how he could be sure that Jesus had entered his life. I read a verse to Cyrus: "Behold, I stand at the door and knock. If anyone hears my voice and opens the door, I will come into him …" (Revelation 3:20, ESV).

"Would Jesus lie to you?" I asked.

"No!" retorted Cyrus.

"You opened the door of your life, so where is Jesus right now?" I queried.

"Is he in my life?" he offered.

"Yes, and how do you know that?" I probed.

"It's written here, in the Bible," Cyrus said, pointing to the verse.

"Yes, Cyrus, that's right. And because it's written in the Bible, you can be sure you have been born again."

We had a follow-on discussion about the love, joy, peace, forbearance, and the other traits that are fruits of the Spirit in a believer's life. It was a beautiful conversation.

On Saturday afternoon, the class members paired up with a staffer to go out into the neighborhood. I paired up with Cyrus. I was taking a brand-new Jesus follower out to make more Jesus followers.

Let's be real: Putting "shoes on the gospel," as the saying goes, by going door-to-door is scary for most Jesus followers (and it was for this staffer too!). However, putting classroom training into practice is when it can make a lasting difference. In the stress of the moment, one tends to grab for everything that was taught, enabling the training to stick. Overcoming nervousness to talk to someone about Christ is an experience that builds faith.

As we went door-to-door, we would ask the resident for their opinion of *The Four Spiritual Laws*. In the States, we used a "community religious survey" to break the ice, but in Africa there is no interpersonal ice. We could jump right in.

At house number one, Cyrus took the lead. The resident invited us in, and Cyrus began to read the booklet to her. But he was excited and read through the entire booklet almost in one breath, without giving the person time to respond. I helped Cyrus back up and re-read the questions, but this lady was already a Jesus follower.

At house number two, Cyrus was rattled and asked if I could take the lead. Again, the resident asked us in, and I began to read the booklet to her. However, she pulled out written material from a religious sect that contradicted the Bible. After some discussion, it appeared we were not making progress, so we thanked her for her time and moved on.

At house number three, Cyrus told me, "I see how to do it now," and he took the lead. We were invited in; Africans are so hospitable. This time Cyrus was more relaxed, and he gave the interested lady time to respond when we came to the questions. She said, yes, she would like for Christ to be on the throne of her life. So, Cyrus led her through the prayer to receive Christ. We were all three elated!

When we got back to the school, the place was in an uproar. All the seminar participants were describing, at the same time, the thrilling things that had taken place and the conversions that had happened. The trainees had met with sixty neighborhood residents and well over half had prayed to receive Christ. The trainees were so excited they could not sit still.

Back at his home later that night, Cyrus asked his wife to read *The Four Spiritual Laws* booklet with him. She immediately became angry. She said she already was a Christian, but being defensive usually means something spiritual is missing. She relented and, sure enough, as Cyrus read her the booklet, she realized she also wanted Jesus as the Lord of her life. So Cyrus led his wife in the prayer to receive Christ. In the weeks to come, I followed up with Cyrus to ensure he understood his new faith, just as Wayne had followed up with me.

The timing of the LIFE seminar was redeeming: Two weeks before I had been ready to give up. But we went out in faith with a group of everyday people, from lesser-known churches, and God put his hand on them. Once again, the ordinary produced the extraordinary when placed in the service of Jesus.

After the LIFE seminar, I recorded in my journal that "I'm at peace. God seems to be using me. He seems very near."

Lost, Not Found

Everyone on the team had a camera. Every Crusade staffer headed overseas simply had to have a 35mm single-lens reflex camera. A major activity during training in California was to select and purchase just the right one. I bought mine used from a senior staffer for one hundred dollars and the seller threw in a telephoto lens as well—a tremendous bargain even then. It was a beautiful device: a Minolta with a totally black body instead of the chrome trim that was the norm. It was my most prized possession.

My Minolta took beautiful pictures. My favorite shots were landscapes taken late in the day, when the shadows were long, using Kodak Ektachrome film that brought out the blues and greens.

We carried our cameras everywhere. We learned that getting a selection of a few good pictures meant "burning" a lot of film. I was once accused on a business trip of being with the CIA because of the number of pictures I took. In fact, we heard rumors several times speculating we were with the CIA. Why else would Americans come to the outback of Bophu?

In a prayer letter, I wrote about children's fascination with a clicking camera. Tswana youth seemed to enjoy having their picture taken even if they never received a copy. Why? I don't know; it was a cross-cultural puzzle. Maybe they thought they'd be on American TV.

On a walk through town, Mike and I were carrying our cameras on our shoulder straps and met a Tswana boy who asked to have his picture taken by the Americans. This was fine; he was really cute. Almost immediately, some friends appeared who also wanted their pictures taken. Then, we looked up to see several hundred children in their black-and-white uniforms rushing over from a nearby school. We turned off the cameras but went through the motion of snapping pictures of the shouting, handwaving throng surrounding us. We picked up the pace of our walk.

Every week or so, someone on the team had a roll of 35mm slides developed, then we had a night of popcorn and slide viewing using a projector and a sheet on the wall. We would "ooh" and "ah" over triumphs of composition and laugh at the bloopers. Through the many slide shows, we probably viewed several thousand pictures between us.

Photography, food, and Risk were our most frequent pastimes, as I noted in my journal:

> *John & Lynn and Duane, Bonnie, Nancy, and Ann were over tonight and we had a good time looking at slides.*
>
> *I cooked up two of the taco dinners [from home] and invited the girls down for supper one nite. We dressed like Mexicans with mascara mustaches and Joe played his Tijuana Brass tape. "Bill's Taco Tavern" we called it.*
>
> *Risk game tonight with Alex & Mike. Good game—Alex won. Cindy flexed and moved family nite to Saturday so we could play.*

Playing Risk was almost addictive. We developed a version using two boards and new rules including navies, airlifts, and playing as two opposing alliances. Games took hours to conclude. Winning strategies were re-hashed for days afterward.

Sometime during the third week of February, I realized I could not find my camera in the kombi, or the house, or anywhere else. We had taken a trip to Johannesburg, and I wondered if I had left it in the Mafikeng convenience store where we stopped on our return. But the shop owner said it had not been found there. I inquired with the police and ran an ad in the Mafikeng newspaper. No response ever came.

Because of import duties, purchasing a 35mm camera in South Africa cost twice as much as in the States, equal to more than a month of my Crusade salary. Having one sent from home would be subject to the same duties and likewise expensive. So thereafter, I watched others record their time in Africa and I got copies of their pictures.

My black-body Minolta had been a fixture in my life, and its mysterious disappearance was discouraging. In my journal, I noted I was "really down about it." However, in a letter home in April, I wrote prophetically, "I'm not in a rush to get a new camera. I just want to wait on the Lord and see what He'll provide."

Every Spreading Tree

With my boss de Wet preoccupied with his move, I began on my own to dig into my new role organizing the equipment of the Department of Works. The Bible says that ancient Israel had idols "on every high hill and under every spreading tree" (2 Kings 17:10). I recognized an analogy to that passage: equipment was strewn across the dusty hills and under the thorn trees in every region of Bophu.

The homeland had inherited its equipment from South Africa's Ministry of Native Affairs when Bophu was made independent. The Imperial Reserve had a file room with a row of metal cabinets containing a brown kraft-paper folder for each piece of equipment the homeland owned. In addition to road and construction equipment, there were files for stationary equipment such as generators (as the rural hospitals used) or pumps for boreholes (water wells).

For mobile equipment, the files were intended to receive a report form submitted monthly on the equipment's location and use. Some files were current because a crew foreman was faithfully submitting the form to the head office. Other files had not seen reports submitted in decades; the location and condition of much of the equipment were unknown. After struggling to make sense of the files, I finally decided the only way to sort this out was to go out and find the stuff.

My daily process was to check out a car from the government motor pool in the morning, grab a map, and travel to locations where equipment was supposedly being used. I might find a motor grader here, a roller there, a broken tractor at this school, a dump truck at that gravel pit, sometimes where it was supposed to be, but often not. Whenever I drove down a rural road, I was on the lookout for abandoned equipment out in a field or under a thorn tree; it was often government property. Almost every government building had some piece of equipment nearby, maybe stationary like a borehole pump, or maybe some sort of rolling stock. Much of it had not been accounted for in years.

As I located the equipment, I noted the physical condition. Equipment that was broken, even with minor issues like a flat tire, might stand idle for months. The inefficiency and disorganization were appalling; thousands of rand were being wasted.

Because of the disarray, equipment was not available to serve the public for, say, keeping a dirt road passable. A road detour cost the public time and expensive fuel. The financial waste from disabled equipment meant that urgent needs, such as a hospital generator, had to wait in line for funding. While the department could hire Johannesburg engineers for many technical needs, it needed someone motivated, committed, and organized to sort out this dilapidated corner of the government. This was an opportunity to tangibly improve the lives of the people we had come to serve.

In the wrinkled files and rusty metal, I discovered the other page of my mission in Africa, the page in which I contributed to the physical needs of the people. I couldn't heal the sick or feed five thousand as Jesus did; instead, he called me to get machinery back to work. I could do that.

Getting a Grip

Each piece of equipment in the files was assigned a unique identifier: the letters YB, *ya Bophuthatswana*, of Bophuthatswana, followed by a sequence of numbers. The equipment could be identified by its manufacturer's serial number, but generally the YB number was faded out or missing altogether. Government property could be innocently misidentified as privately owned or was fair game for thieves.

So after finding a piece of equipment, it needed to be clearly marked with its YB number. I investigated adhesive labels or stamped metal plates, but both ideas had supply problems. In the end, I took the simple route and decided to mark the equipment with yellow paint.

At home, I used a razor-blade knife to cut out cardboard stencils for the letters YB and multiple sets of numbers. I began to mark every piece of equipment I found with its YB number, a laborious process. I also enlisted a file clerk to find and mark equipment. We went through many cans of paint.

I wrote home in May that I was also investigating automating the inventory.

> *Started working this week on learning how to program Bophu's finance computer to handle our inventory of heavy equipment.*
>
> *They have brought in a Swiss chap to run the computer programming and he is very sharp. He is preparing a program to inventory and print monthly operating statistics for the heavy equipment. However, I wonder if it will really be much help.*

The automation effort was admirable, but I was right to be dubious. It took almost a year to get to the data-entry stage.

By the end of May, after almost four months of locating and marking equipment and updating the files, I was able to justify buying a magnetic board divided into regions that enabled the department to visually see where the mobile equipment was located. We could then reallocate it around the country where most needed and keep tabs on equipment that needed repair.

Colored magnets and stencils cut out on the kitchen floor were a humble start, but they gave the department a grip on a big problem.

Reaching Out

In April, Mike and I started a Bible study at work that provided me with much-needed experience in ministry. After four months, I wrote in a journal entry:

> *Have got a couple of fireballs, one is from Mike's church, the other went to the Vision Conference and is an African gospel [an African who personifies the good news of Jesus].*

Also in April, I joined Bonnie to teach a Bible study at Barolong High School. In May, I recorded in my journal:

> *After work, Bonnie and I headed to Barolong for Bible Study. The four guys that were there last week were back plus four new guys—all of whom prayed to receive Christ.*

The students were always eager, but attendance was erratic. One week I might have eight students show up; the next week there might be one. Nevertheless, by July I reported I had three "chaps" that I was meeting with consistently at Barolong. During this time, I also began a long effort to establish a group at a local trade school named Boitseanape Technical Secondary School.

A significant portion of the rural population, such as in the villages around Montshiwa, could not read. The team developed a picture booklet for sharing the good news with non-readers based on a booklet that was already in use in Kenya. The booklet used pictures of a father and son to illustrate the relationship between man and our heavenly Father. The story of the good news of Jesus was explained like this:

On the cover, the son was humbly holding his hands up to the father, who was kissing them. This illustrated a father blessing his son, a powerful African image. This represents the love our heavenly Father has for each of us.

The first page after the cover had a picture of a gorge separating the father and the son, and the son was walking away with his back turned to the father. This illustrates sin, man's fundamental obedience problem in which we choose to go our own way. Sin separates us from God.

The next picture showed the gorge spanned by a bridge with Jesus's cross over it. The son was stepping onto the bridge to cross over to his beckoning father. This illustrates that Jesus can solve man's sin problem by providing the path to God through his death for our sins.

Next was a picture of the son accepting a gift from the father and kneeling in prayer. This illustrates the gift of salvation. This is when a person acknowledges sin and invites Christ into his or her life as Lord.

On the back cover, the father and the son were seated, and the son was listening to the father teach him from a book. This signifies the ongoing fellowship between a Jesus follower and God the Father in personal growth.

With an accompanying verbal explanation, the pictures provided the guidance needed to become a Jesus follower. Neither the Jesus follower explaining the booklet nor the recipient hearing the message needed to be literate.

Here's Life

From our earliest days in Bophu, we had been discussing a community-wide outreach called "Here's Life," also known by its slogan "I Found It." It was described as a movement "working through local churches with the goal of giving everyone in their community an opportunity to find new life in Jesus Christ." It had been used in 246 US cities in the mid-seventies, and millions across America had become Jesus followers as a result. I participated in the Birmingham campaign. The concept had been used in Europe, the Philippines, and Kenya, and it was introduced in southern Africa in a Swaziland campaign in early 1978.

I mentioned Here's Life in a letter home in May. The event, at that time, was scheduled only six months away.

> *We're gearing up for our Here's Life campaign in Montshiwa/Mafikeng in October. I've been put in charge of the training and mass media materials.*

Given that Here's Life was a communication event, I had a lot to plan, develop, and print as media coordinator: tracts, posters, banners, bumper stickers, and even pin-on buttons. The media included campaign jingles to be played from a loudspeaker mounted on a sound truck that would make circuits through the neighborhoods of Montshiwa. A series of tape-recorded lessons for training church members would be translated into Setswana. A response system would be developed to tabulate the results of the campaign.

The campaign objective was to completely saturate Montshiwa and its surrounding villages. The population of this area was 90,000 to 100,000 souls. In hindsight, it's implausible that fourteen inexperienced foreigners could have an impact on such a large and widespread audience. It was bold and not a little crazy.

And it was a lot of hard work too.

Chapter 14

THE CONSPIRACY

I learned much about following Jesus from the interaction with my teammates. The book of Proverbs has a verse for this process:

> As iron sharpens iron,
> so one man sharpens another. (Proverbs 27:17)

But the rasping of an iron file can be painful.

March 10

Tonight, we had team meeting at Steve & Duane's. We listened to a [Larry] Poland tape based on Romans 8:28. Poland described how we are all caught in a "conspiracy of circumstances" arranged by our Father for our good.

I've begun to see myself in such a conspiracy. I'm caught in a foreign culture with a small group of people from my home culture with whom I must work closely. No longer are my habits hide-able; no longer can I be a recluse without the group noting it ... And this is of course why God arranged the conspiracy—to bring about a change for my good.

Larry Poland was the director of the Agape Ministry and a widely known speaker. Poland's concept of a "conspiracy of circumstances" has many applications. In late March, I recorded in my journal an incident involving my conspiracy.

My teammates and I had access to the tennis courts in the parliament compound, near President Mangope's house, and about a mile from our house in Montshiwa. In this incident, Joe organized the games in a way that offended me. So I picked up my racket, opened the gate, and walked home. I was hyper-sensitive because of a vulnerability related to sports. I referred to it in a journal entry during the staff conference the previous December.

> *Today is social afternoon; games & recreation etc. Bophu is playing Swazi in football. But I bowed out. The most important potential I didn't develop as a kid was athletic.*

There are many selfish defenses for a weakness among the sons of Adam: some get angry, some attack, some implode. My version of defense in this incident was to withdraw. I retreated into myself, but I found that I could not walk with God inside a shell. My conscience ached.

I would not have been offended by someone who was also a klutz, but then my weakness would have gone unhealed. Instead, God designed a conspiracy of circumstances to deal with my problem. It was not accidental that I came to have a roommate, Joe, who was a collegiate-sport-playing, scholarship-winning athlete, whereas I was, well, the opposite. Yet God knew there could be no better person for me to trust with my vulnerability than my spiritual roommate, Joe. I just needed to be humble enough to do so. I recorded the resolution in my journal:

> *After a few days of disobedience, I just stepped into Joe's room, told him I had to talk with him and then asked his forgiveness for being such a clod about the tennis game last Thursday nite. It was one of the hardest things I've ever had to set my will to do.*

Jesus told his disciples, "Whoever loses his life for my sake will find it" (Matthew 10:39). This is a great paradox: Jesus says the only way to find our life is to first lose it for his sake. There is a related passage by the apostle Paul: "If by the Spirit you put to death the misdeeds of the body, you will live" (Romans 8:13). Pastor Barker once told me that growing in

Christ means dying to self, that is, dying to self's preference for its own way instead of God's way.

In another rasping of iron on iron, I recognized that the life lived to satisfy self doesn't die quietly:

> *Today Joe & I kinda got cross with each other ... the best thing is for me to approach him and ask forgiveness & talk it out. But that is hard to do; whenever self must die it is a hard thing.*

Pastor Barker said that dying to self is often painful. My journal entry about apologizing to Joe noted that killing off my old selfish nature hurts. C. S. Lewis wrote about pain:

> We are not merely imperfect creatures who must be improved: we are, as Newman said, rebels who must lay down our arms. The first answer, then, to the question of why our cure should be painful, is that to render back the will which we have so long claimed for our own, is in itself, wherever and however it is done, a grievous pain.[1]

Pain has a purpose. In the physical body, it warns of a malfunction that must be attended to. In this incident, emotional pain warned of an unhealthy sensitivity, which could not be avoided in my particular conspiracy of circumstances. Because of the pain of dying to self for Jesus's sake, I found authentic life, rather than continuing as a poser.

Not a Bunch of Parts

It would be hard to overstate the impact we teammates had on each other spiritually.

> *Tonight Bonnie came over and she, Joe, Mike & I had a big pow-wow about our vocations and more importantly our attitudes toward them. All of us face ridiculous, frustrating situations. It is easy to complain and gripe. But we all acknowledged we've sinned in our words, often setting others alight so they sinned too. We prayed about it and it was really good to confess to each other and seek God's solutions together.*

> *God has really given me a sense of identity with the team. I need them and vice versa and have realized that we are a body and not a bunch of parts.*

Living in honest, close Christian fellowship is a powerful stimulus for personal growth—motivation to truly change from the inside. C. S. Lewis wrote about fellowship:

> Christ, who said to the disciples, "Ye have not chosen me, but I have chosen you," can truly say to every group of Christian friends, "You have not chosen one another but I have chosen you for one another."[2]

Amid this period of struggle and growth, God provided refreshment: his version of the "USO."

> *June 12*
>
> *Tonight, the Smite ministry singers sang at Bophelong. They were an excellent singing group based with Liberty Baptist College in Lynchburg, Va. It was so refreshing talking to Americans again. I know how soldiers must feel at the U.S.O. The girls were cute and talkative. Quite a few southerners in the group, even a girl from Birmingham & Mobile [Alabama].*
>
> *Thanx, Lord, for tonite. For a fresh breeze from home. For loving us so much.*

Performance

Pastor Ron Dunn frames the connection between the inner life and outer performance when he asks, "Are you free to fail?" Can we accept failure as part of God's plan, or do we worship success?

In early June, I recorded in my journal that I attended a meeting in which Secretary Masibi expressed high regard for the accomplishments of my two teammate engineers; he used the expression "fitting in like a glove." There I sat, but no comment was made about my contribution. To me, the omission was deafening. Later in the month, I again did not meet expectations.

The Conspiracy

Each year, the South African government had a "tender" process, a request for quotations from suppliers, that was used to create a catalog of vehicles at prescribed prices. Bophu government agencies had access to this catalog, but a justification, or "motivation," had to be prepared to secure the budget for the purchase. My opening foray into procurement was writing a motivation for Toyota lorries (trucks).

Besides the budget motivation, another critical work task was due the same week.

June 29 (letter home)

My job with the gov't continues to be tough. Petrol & diesel prices are so high [due to the Arab oil embargo] that we had to write an explanation to the President for why we needed our mobile equipment. It's taken all week and meanwhile other pressing things have had to wait.

And in a further stress point, the coming weekend was a vision conference for our Here's Life campaign. The team had worked hard to urge local pastors to come. As media coordinator, I had a big stake in this meeting. In my letter home I noted:

This weekend we have our "vision" conference or orientation meeting to explain the Here's Life strategy to pastors and church leaders. We have about 50 people coming. There are also some pastors coming up from Swaziland to tell what happened in their churches as a result of the 1978 Swaziland Here's Life campaign.

After a strained work week, and then a full weekend with the conference, Monday brought bad news. I wrote in my journal on July 2:

Work was the pits today. Masibi rejected my motivation on the lorries. Asked for prayer at the team meeting tonite but felt so silly and emotional. Lots of other folks are 'down' and I feel like I'm dragging the team down.

The team members may have been "down" with plain exhaustion from putting on a big conference. In addition, the conference attendance

125

was not what we hoped. For example, Joe, Bonnie, and I had met in person with the pastor of our church to deliver an invitation, but he didn't come. Further, several teammates were having serious problems with their vocational assignments.

As I expressed at the team meeting, my work performance had brought me a feeling of failure. Christian counselor and author Bill Ewing writes:

> Though unique to each individual, the personal standards or demands we create are just as real and carry the same heavy consequences of any law derived from Scriptures, society, or religion. They become most obvious when we "blow it" and cannot do or be what we feel we must in order to be acceptable.[3]

Depending on "the personal standards or demands we create" to obtain inner peace is a recipe for either frustration when we fail, or pride when we succeed. If success is a person's source of inner peace, that person will be flattened by failure.

In contrast, the Bible teaches that our inner condition is a product of walking in the Spirit of God: "But the fruit of the Spirit is love, joy, peace …" (Galatians 5:22). God's joy and peace are available in both life's wins and losses.

Besides machines and media, I was in Africa for God to build within me a new depth of faith. God brings us to the end of our rope, so we will trust him. He knew that when I was free to fail, I could enjoy being me.

July 14

This weekend is a team retreat … It's been on leadership and has been a blessing. I've learned a lot. Played volleyball and football this afternoon. As usual, I did poorly, but enjoyed it anyhow. Sometimes my pride hardens me, but I'm seeing how futile and hypocritical that is.

In mathematics, an inflection point occurs when the slope of a curve changes. It is used outside of math for any occasion of significant change.

July 1979 was an inflection month. Going forward, God's work in my life produced journal entries that were less sensitive and more sensible. Not perfect, you understand, but noticeably less imperfect.

The Glimmer

July 22 (letter home)
I've come to the point where I see how this crazy government works and I'm friends with the right people to get things done. More and more, people are bringing their equipment problems to me. This is reassuring because they must think I can help them ...

Much of our heavy equipment was old—hand-me-downs from the South African government. One of the government's workshop managers had arranged to send a ten-year-old bulldozer to a Johannesburg vendor for repair. After the fact, it was not clear what scope of work the workshop manager had asked the vendor to perform. In any case, the vendor took the initiative to completely dismantle the behemoth, every nut and bolt down to the frame, and then he prepared a quote to overhaul it. The quote was twenty-five thousand rand (over ninety thousand in today's dollars), a significant fraction of what a new machine would cost. The workshop manager asked me what he should do. He may well have been surprised by the price tag.

One thing I had learned about heavy equipment is that a machine's frame fatigues—that is, sags—after years of operation. At that point, the equipment can be difficult to maintain and operate. Was the machine at this point? Hard to say. I took this problem to Mr. Botha, and the huge rugby player leaned back and said something to the effect of, *"Auk mon,* this is when you earn your money," not knowing how little I was living on!

Providentially, a friend from Birmingham sent a methodology for determining the best time to trade in heavy equipment. My figures said the cost to reassemble the bulldozer was not economical. I made that recommendation to Mr. Pretorius who had the final say. Over the protests of the workshop manager, the dozer was scrapped.

The department subsequently had a meeting to establish a policy concerning expensive overhauls. My analysis indicated it was often better to buy new machines rather than invest in obsolete ones. By this time, we had a new manager at the Mafikeng workshop, a fellow named Le Roux, and he sided with me. The deputy secretary of works decreed that, in the future, major repairs would have to be approved by the head office. And he delegated the approval authority to me.

I began to sense in my work a glimmer of something that had been more foreign than thorn trees: respect. I now knew a great deal about the government's equipment situation. People called and said they needed my opinion, and I actually had one. My answer served better than the vacuum that existed otherwise (albeit, the bar was low). It was gratifying, yet humbling. God had walked with me through some dark valleys to get here.

In late July, we had another LIFE training seminar. We hoped that this event would spark a commitment from churches to participate in the Here's Life campaign. We went far and wide to invite pastors to attend. Joe and I even went to distant villages. I noted in a July letter home, "If our Here's Life campaign is to 'go' this October, the pastors and laymen who attend the LIFE are going to have to catch the vision for it."

But vision-catching proved elusive. The Here's Life schedule was pushed off from October to February of the next year, and then to March.

Found, Not Lost

Sometime in late June, the team was invited to a social gathering with some of our local ministry friends. I was talking with one of these friends and the topic turned to photography. I related that I had owned a 35mm black-body Minolta, but I had lost it several months ago. My friend remarked how interesting, because he had recently met someone in Mafikeng who had a 35mm black-body Minolta. My friend noted that this "camera person" (for want of a better name) was a little vague about how he came by such a unique camera. I got his name and where he worked.

The next day I went to the South African police station in Mafikeng with the clipping of the ad I had run in the newspaper and the camera's serial number. I explained the situation and a police officer was assigned to look into it. We drove over to meet with "camera person."

The white police officer and camera person, also white, had a spirited discussion in Afrikaans during which the tall police officer glared down at camera person. I could not follow the words, but the body language was clear. After a few tense minutes, camera person abruptly turned and walked to the back of his workplace. When he came back, he was carrying a camera case, which he turned over to the police officer. The officer handed it to me to identify it. I opened the case to find a 35mm black-body Minolta. The serial number matched; it was mine. I was holding a miracle in my hands.

Camera person offered no apology or explanation. I assume I had absentmindedly set the camera down four months before during our stop at the Mafikeng convenience store, and camera person picked it up and walked away with it.

The South African police force administered the laws of apartheid, and policemen could be strict and severe, to put it mildly. As an expatriate, I could have been put off or ignored. I had no particular rights to fair dealing. However, the small-town police officer was professional and closed the camera incident simply and quietly. I was profusely thankful to my tall benefactor, who expressed the indispensable *auk* and modestly shrugged.

I was also thankful to the One in heaven who enjoys amazing us.

Chapter 15

THE VELD

VELD, AFRIKAANS: GRASSLAND OR SAVANNAH.
PRONOUNCED: FELT.

I had traveled through most of Bophu in my first ten months. I'd been to parched and sparsely populated Kuruman, 301 kilometers to the west of the Imperial Reserve; to Thaba 'Nchu, the isolated mountain region near Lesotho, 495 kilometers to the south; and to heavily populated *Ga-Rankuwa* (gah ran COO wuh) on the outskirts of Pretoria, 286 kilometers to the east. The land had beauty, but it wore a veil.

Bophu was located on the high central plain of southern Africa. It had the latitude of Miami, but at an elevation of 1,200 meters (4,000 feet), it had a temperature profile more like the southeastern US: hot summers and cold but not extreme winters. The Bophu summer heat had low humidity and in that regard was more tolerable than, say, Alabama. In the Bophu winter, mornings had an occasional frost, while further south (and cooler since it's further from the equator), Thaba 'Nchu might have a snowfall.

The climate of the central plain of South Africa is dry—it is bordered to the northwest by the Kalahari, the great desert of southern Africa. The rainfall is sufficient to grow *mielies* (corn), but there is plenty of dust caught up in the atmosphere during the windy dry spells. The predominant natural flora is the wheat-straw-colored grass. There are cypress trees in the towns and willows along the streams, but no trees break up the grass stretching to the horizon except for the flat-topped thorn trees. From the border with Botswana in the north to the foothills of the Drakensberg Mountains in the south, the land is a vast savannah—the South African *veld*.

The veld is much like the prairies of the US, the pampas of Argentina, or the steppe of Russia. The most prominent feature is that it's flat, and in some places, very flat. At night in those very flat areas, the lights of the town ahead can be seen for thirty kilometers standing flat-footed on the highway. In other places, one finds a slight roll to the land and the occasional ridge of *koppies* (hills or knolls).

The veld shares a characteristic with other savannahs: the wind. The wind of the veld is like an ongoing conversation with a temperamental live-in boarder; it can range from a friendly chat to a fierce intrusion, but rarely is it silent.

When we told Americans living in other areas of South Africa where we lived, the usual response was, "Well, at least you have the sunsets." And they were right. Our dusty lane pointed directly toward the western horizon, where each evening we were simultaneously blinded by the setting sun and awed by another sunset in Bophuthatswana.

The dust in the air of the veld splits the sun's light like a prism into every possible shade of red, yellow, and orange. Any wisps of clouds add brush strokes of pink and purple. The combination of these colors with the sweeping view of the horizon and the piercing topaz of the African sky yields glorious sunsets.

The color-filled display starts at the horizon and gradually advances up into the blue overhead as the shimmering white orb slides down into the thicker portion of the atmosphere and melts into the distant edge of the veld. Silhouetted out on the veld are the iconic thorn trees, and at the horizon the grass itself glows as if afire as the last golden rays of the sun pierce through it.

The veld itself is not so dramatic. After greening up in the spring, the knee-high grass settles into its dull wheat-straw color through the other seasons of the year. We often heard South Africans talk in affectionate terms of the veld, but we couldn't see the magic. The veld held nothing to commend; it was kilometer after kilometer of sameness.

It was on a night drive to Thaba 'Nchu when the veld magic touched me. The road was long and straight and slightly elevated above the veld, which was its uniform sameness 360 degrees around my little government car speeding through the night. The moon above was so bright that the car cast a shadow. A gusty wind shifted it from time to time.

Then I saw it. With the silver hue of the moon illuminating the veld, a wave crashed against the shoulder of the roadway. And then another, and another. A succession of waves broke, and the rollers stretched out beyond my window at an angle to the road, running deep into the veld, as far as I could see. The heads of the veld grass were dipping in unison to the wind, moving as what they really were: a sea. A dry yet fluid sea.

It took little imagination to feel the car become a ship riding the waves on an inland ocean. I anchored my craft for a moment, stepped ashore, and the sea breeze warmed my face as wave after wave rolled across the veld.

The veld was never the same after that night. I saw in it something simple and humble—a blade of grass—but I also saw vast grandeur because the veld grass responding to the wind was beyond counting or numbering. I saw in the veld how God's humility and his majesty are revealed in creation.

For the Creator God is so humble as to be born as a baby like every other human child, and yet he is so majestic as to have flung a billion galaxies into space with stars beyond counting or numbering.

And so, in this way, the magic of the veld taught me about the nature of God.

So wyd as die Heer se genade,
   As vast as the mercy of God,
le die veld in sterlig en skade.[1]
   lies the veld in starlight and shadow.

                    —Eugene Marais

Chapter 16

INTERLUDE: THE ELEPHANT OUTSIDE THE ROOM

Much has been written about the racial and political setting in South Africa forty years ago. The books, reports, articles, and dissertations could fill a fair-sized library. Hopefully, the limited overview that follows will enable the reader to understand the context of our calling.

To ensure there is no confusion, I must emphasize that the history that follows is exactly that—history. South Africa has been majority-ruled since 1994. The country went through an extensive and painful process at that time to heal wounds and re-establish governing institutions. Now, an entire generation has grown up in South Africa free of apartheid.

By almost any measure of development, South Africa in the late 1970s was far beyond any other country in Africa. Spurred by embargoes and other restrictions on trade, it had developed an impressive independence in many manufactured goods as well as in advanced technologies, including nuclear power and atomic weapons. To make up for its lack of oil, the homegrown chemical company SASOL developed processes to convert South Africa's abundant coal to liquid fuels. The papers talked of plans to locally manufacture diesel engines, which at the time were imported.

South Africa's industry grew from its mines. As Saudi Arabia is for oil, so South Africa is for minerals. Historian Frank Welsh notes:

> The country was, after all, one of the world's richest sources of minerals, among the first three in alumino-silicates,

chrome, manganese, platinum, titanium, vanadium—and possibly uranium—together with gold, of which it was still the world's biggest producer.[1]

As for infrastructure, South African Railways was efficient and provided rail service even in black-ruled countries well to the north. The ports at Cape Town, Port Elizabeth, and Durban were major entry points for goods into the continent. The road system was modern, paved, and well maintained. Although South Africa represented only a small percentage of the continent's population, it generated more than half of its electricity.

Besides infrastructure and industry, South Africa led Africa in other measures, such as adult literacy. The salaries and living conditions of blacks in South Africa were in the main superior to the rest of the sub-Saharan continent. Welsh writes:

> Compared with the rest of Africa, even after decades of oppression, South Africa could claim to be in the lead. Attempting to measure the unmeasurable, the United Nations Human Development Index placed South Africa at the head of all African countries ...[2]

Why, then, was there so much discontent among the non-white population? Nelson Mandela once noted that black South Africans did not compare themselves to citizens of other countries; they compared their situation to that of white South Africans. And the disparity in that comparison was institutionalized by the system of apartheid.

Grand Apartheid

Apartheid began shortly after the Nationalist Party won a majority of the seats in the South African parliament in 1948. This was a whites-only election, except for a limited franchise to non-whites in the Cape province. To gain control of the country, the Nationalist Party only had to win a majority of the white vote; the non-white population had no say in the outcome.

The voting franchise in South Africa was prescribed by the 1910 constitution that ended the British colonial period and established the

Interlude: The Elephant Outside the Room

Union of South Africa as a sovereign nation. The British parliament approved the constitution, which did not provide for universal voting rights. Racial segregation existed under Dutch and British rule, but their laws were restrained compared to the legal leviathan the Nationalists would create.

The objective of generations of Afrikaner leaders was to be rid of English domination. When the Nationalist Party, controlled by Afrikaner politicians, won control of parliament, they effectively accomplished that goal. They moved swiftly to consolidate their power and also to institute "Grand Apartheid," which was their solution to the "native problem." It was ironic that the oppressed would become oppressors.

One of the first legislative acts passed by the Nationalist-controlled parliament was to delineate four distinct racial groups: black, white, Coloured (people of mixed race), and Indian (descendants of Indian, Malaysian, and other Asian immigrants). It's important to understand that the term "Coloured" in apartheid South Africa referred to a racial classification. It did not have the same use or meaning as the word "colored" in historical US race relations.

Every South African citizen was assigned to one of the four racial classifications based on ancestry or physical characteristics. Living areas were prescribed for each group by the Group Areas Act (1950). When this law was implemented, it brought gut-wrenching upheaval to many. Photo essayist Eugene Cole notes:

> Since the law went into effect the Nationalist Government has carved the face of South Africa into a racial checkerboard of airtight black, white, Coloured, and Indian squares. Hundreds of thousands of people have been uprooted in the process.[3]

Additional laws passed by the Nationalists racially segregated public facilities—for example, buses and trains, schools and hospitals, and even park benches, elevators, and bus stops. A color bar was established reserving classes of jobs for whites, and another law prohibited mixed marriages. Blacks had to carry a much-hated "pass book," similar to a passport, signed by an employer, to legally be allowed in a "white" area.

Reservations for each of the black tribes, known as homelands, had been established in the British colonial period. However, the amount of land set aside in the homelands was never proportional to the black population: only 13 percent of the land of South Africa was contained in tribal homelands for 70 percent of the population. Predictably, the majority of blacks could not find work in their homeland and moved to be near the large cities. Over 60 percent of the Tswana, although citizens of the homeland of Bophuthatswana, lived and worked outside Bophu borders as quasi-permanent residents of white areas.[4]

The primary foundation underlying apartheid was a concept called "Separate Development." The basis of this theory was that each tribe and each race constituted a separate "nation" that should mature and progress independently.

However theorized, Separate Development had an enormous gap to address. Just as with the quantity of land, every measure of the quality of life for non-whites—income, economic opportunity, education, protection of families, health care, infant mortality, etc.—was inferior, and in most instances abysmally inferior, to that of the ruling minority. In black residential areas, sanitation was rudimentary, electrification minimal, and roads largely unpaved. Apartheid in and of itself did not introduce any efficiencies capable of overcoming this development gap. Instead, the administration of apartheid imposed an economic and manpower burden on South Africa.

Nothing to Lose

The apartheid policy generated intense opposition. The most prominent apartheid resistance organization in 1979 was the African National Congress (ANC), but it had been banned and its leaders, such as Nelson Mandela, were jailed or forced underground. In addition, a plethora of lesser-known activist groups fought against apartheid. A vocal but outnumbered white opposition in the South African parliament argued with pro-apartheid whites.

Acts of sabotage and violence by anti-apartheid groups kept the population on edge and police and security forces on alert. Thousands of young men had secretly left South Africa to join liberation armies that

INTERLUDE: THE ELEPHANT OUTSIDE THE ROOM

were based in neighboring countries.

However, it would be incorrect to think that opposition to apartheid was solidly united. If the opposition of the Zulu-led Inkatha party to the Xhosa-led ANC party is taken as an example, the black tribes were divided. Welsh explains that "older antagonisms between the ANC, often perceived as a Xhosa organization, and Buthelezi's Zulu Inkatha supporters began to rekindle, especially in Natal ..."[5]

The Afrikaans-speaking whites were approximately 60 percent of the white population.[6] The remainder of the whites were descended from English-speaking immigrants primarily from Britain. South Africa was often portrayed as a straightforward white versus black crisis, but in reality, the whites were also divided. Welsh writes:

> One survey in 1977, after [the 1976 riots in] Soweto, showed that 78 percent of Afrikaners supported a "consensus policy of apartheid", a view shared by only 25 percent of English speakers, although it has to be said that a much higher proportion consistently took advantage of the benefits of such a policy.[7]

Whites versus non-whites, whites versus whites, blacks versus whites, blacks versus blacks, and "Indian" and "Coloured" peoples with their own objectives—the political complexity was bewildering.

A white acquaintance once asked me this blunt question, "Why is South Africa such a stench in the nostrils of the US? After all, you killed off your natives." I don't remember how I responded, but I should have pointed out that we forced our "natives," the American Indians, onto reservations much like South Africa was attempting to do. I would confess, and believe most Americans would agree, that it was an abhorrent period in US history.

I would then point out current events in South Africa—for example, the tragedy that occurred on June 13, 1976, in the black township of Soweto, just two years before we arrived in South Africa.

> When police, using machine pistols, fired on a crowd of demonstrating school children, over twenty were killed.

> Photographs of the dead thirteen-year-old Hector Petersen being carried from the scene accompanied by his screaming sister were flashed around the world, arousing universal denunciation: within a few days the UN security council had condemned the South African government and demanded an end to apartheid.[8]

This heartbreaking event was still being heatedly discussed by my black work colleagues at the Imperial Reserve. My white acquaintance did not refer to it—perhaps he missed the evening news that day.

Although my acquaintance was quick to note how America dealt with its "natives," there were never any comments or questions about how America dealt with racial integration. For all its faults, the US was much farther down the path of civil rights than South Africa, which with the introduction of apartheid was going in the opposite direction.

Apartheid bred bitterness, anger, and despair in the non-white populace. To hold the system together, South Africa spent enormous resources on maintaining a near police state for non-whites. The black man lived in fear of this police state. The white man also lived in fear: since he had everything to lose, he rightly feared those who had nothing to lose.

How Did It Come to This?

The injustice of this system should have been obvious. As American missionary Nik Ripken wrote, "The racism that we found in South Africa was racism on steroids, racism multiplied to the nth degree."[9]

Many white South Africans were indeed ashamed of apartheid. White South Africans were responding to the racial problem throughout the country. In our area, white South African teachers and medical professionals were employed by the Bophu government to provide the black leaders with assistance independent of the white South African government.

South African Christians pondered and prayed about how to be God's instrument in the environment in which they found themselves.

Interlude: The Elephant Outside the Room

August 17 (Leadership Dynamics Conference)

Great discussion at my table at the banquet. South African Christians are thinking & questioning trying to find their role in the society Christ has placed them in. They have a great challenge and call to follow Christ here.

But however good the efforts and sentiments of the few, a majority of white South Africans voted for apartheid. Most of the white civil servants in the South African government sincerely believed that separation was the best policy for all the peoples of South Africa. The seconded officials we worked alongside endeavored with good intentions to make this concept a reality. These were decent, hard-working people. *Why did they not see the wretchedness of apartheid?*

In 1978, "apart-ness" had been in place for a generation. South African whites did not have an in-depth association with non-whites; contact was limited to work or domestic labor. There were no cross-racial associations in education, church, sports, or social settings.

There were also cultural differences, as noted previously in regards to family relations. Communication hurdles existed as well; one side of most inter-racial conversations was speaking in their second language. Usually, it was the non-white side.

I once spent the night on one of my equipment safaris with a well-meaning friend, a white South African businessman who was a gemstone trader. He put some light on the situation when he told me, "I have an African gardener that takes care of my lawn. I don't know how to carry on a conversation with him. 'How are the roses?' I could ask. Would he then ask, 'How are the diamonds?' I don't know where to start, and neither would he."

Lack of familiarity—that is, only knowing others superficially—can breed misconceptions and rationalizations. And from there, it is a short walk to selfishness and a lack of compassion.

Racial reconciliation should have weighed on practically every observation and every decision in the troubled country. At the very least, race relations should have been the elephant in the room. But apartheid had pushed the elephant out of the room, and the elephant was angry.

This leads to a root question: how is racial reconciliation to be addressed?

A Third Ministry

I cannot explain what might affect another's perspective, but I can describe how becoming familiar with people who were different from me affected my heart.

During Crusade training in California, I attended a predominantly black church and learned that worship styles could be different and yet enjoyable and uplifting. Living with the Joneses, I saw the family members' daily routine and interactions and I realized that the dynamics of their home life were much the same as mine. Through our close friendship, I learned that race relations had dramatically affected their life choices. The realization that I could be unaware of racial hurdles in my home culture expanded my ability to accept and appreciate others. I have deep gratitude to the Jones family for opening their home and lives.

Similarly, living with Khumo and Faith I learned how an African couple cooked, washed clothes, and got to work on time. We shared with each other what God was teaching us. For all of these similarities, however, there were also marked differences in the structure of life, such as family and tribal relationships. But I realized that these cultural differences, like the worship style in California, were neutral choices, neither right nor wrong.

Khumo and Faith talked candidly about the racial situation. The impact of apartheid was so extreme that, before we lived in her home, Faith did not believe that white and black could live together at all. But when *apartness* was replaced with *closeness*, Faith claimed Mike and me as her new sons. I developed great affection for my African parents.

With my work colleagues—both black and white—we traveled the long flat highways of the veld together and wiped away the dust of Bophu's back roads. Together, we tolerated the acrid fumes of diesel engines and the nauseating stench of sewage. We left work stained yellow with stencil paint. We argued into agreement about how to keep the machines running. We discussed career hopes and fears. They took me into their homes and served mielie pap and savory *boerewors* sausage. We laughed together.

Interlude: The Elephant Outside the Room

These shared experiences washed into oblivion any ethnic or racial rejection I might have felt.

In our Bophu ministry with pastors and laymen, we worked as a team to accomplish a spiritual vision. I saw their dedication to God as they prayed fervently, sang powerfully, and taught the Bible ardently. I saw them stressed and frustrated and also excited and full of joy, just as I was. We worked side-by-side in the heat and dust to witness for Jesus Christ. Even now, I admire their faith, and I hope to emulate their love of God.

One of my most fundamental lessons living and working in these cross-ethnic, cross-cultural, and cross-racial situations was about personalities. We all have the same things driving us. We all have laughs and loves, fears and faults, angst and aspirations. We all love our families, crave respect, and yearn for a better life. I learned that cultural differences can mask these commonalities. But inside, beyond culture, beyond skin color, we are all the same.

From these conclusions, we can extrapolate to a too-often overlooked reality: No explanation of the common traits in our personalities makes sense without a common source. We are all created by one and the same God. How can there be racial discrimination amid this supernatural and undeniable truth?

I can't say what would have bridged the divides created by apartheid. I only know any walls I had were demolished by up-close interactions and by overcoming hardships together. And any doubt of reciprocal affection was erased by the hospitality I so often received.

In some of his last words, Jesus prayed to his heavenly Father for those "you gave me out of the world," that is, all Jesus followers. He prayed that the Father would protect them "so that they may be one as we are one" (John 17:6,11). Jesus expects all believers to have the same closeness with each other that Jesus has with the Father.

With a shared love of Jesus at the center, our relationships do not need to bridge a divide; there ought to be no divide at all, only brotherhood or sisterhood. The apostle Paul wrote, "There is neither Jew nor Greek, slave nor free, male nor female, for you are all one in Christ Jesus" (Galatians 3:28). I can affirm Paul's declaration because I experienced it.

Our band of American messengers had a unique opportunity to demonstrate that Jesus loves each and every race. Within Bophu, the political and legal hurdles of apartheid had been neutralized and to the extent our white skins were cause for suspicion, our American citizenship made us approachable. It was insanely obvious that this opportunity had been arranged by God.

I have described our ministry as two adjacent pages in an open book, spiritual on one side and physical on the other. But we had a third ministry: to demonstrate that different races could share life happily alongside each other. This third ministry was incidental to the other two, but we could not have been successful without it. We fulfilled this third leg of ministry without even knowing it.

A number of years after I had returned to the US, Africa provided the most amazing of its many miraculous surprises. My teammate Ann, who was living in Idaho at the time, by pure, providential chance met a Tswana college student who was attending a US university. This young woman grew up in Montshiwa and was a child when we lived there. Compounding the connection, the young lady had been a student of teammate Bonnie, whose vocational role was a classroom teacher in a Montshiwa school.

The Tswana student told Ann that the entire Montshiwa community was strongly influenced by our decision to live among them. Our lives were on stage for all to observe. They saw that the raucous soccer games their children had in our yards generated smiles and laughter. We greeted them with our smattering of Setswana across our back fences. Through the many interactions of daily life they found that whites could live in harmony with blacks without any strain whatsoever. For a generation raised under the harsh rule of apartheid, this was a radical change in perspective. Just our being there changed the view of many from a belief that racism is a *skin* issue to an understanding that racism is a *heart* issue.

And in that realization is hope. Pigmentation doesn't change, but God can change hearts.

Chapter 17

THE GIFT

The kombi jolted sharply as it bounced into another rut in the donkey-cart trail. Joe was piloting our mechanical donkey cart to a nearby village, which consisted of a mixture of tin-roofed block houses and thatched-roof mud houses. We were in search of water, as back at our government house in Montshiwa, the city water system was out for unknown reasons, and the spigots in our house were dry. We knew that the villages near Montshiwa had water wells, so we had loaded up a galvanized washtub in the back of the kombi and roared off to find one.

After a few miles, we arrived in a village with a classic stone-walled well equipped with a windlass and bucket. Villages might appear to be arranged in a jumble to a Westerner, but every building is thoughtfully located at the direction of the village chief; he has both the prerogative and accountability for the allocation of land.

With a smile and a wave to the villagers standing in the doorways, we proceeded to fill our tub from the well. The villagers were all women and small children standing by their mothers. The men had walked the dusty miles into town to work, and the older children were out herding the goats or cattle belonging to their fathers. The villagers did not respond to our greetings; they watched in stone-faced silence. We shrugged, loaded the full tub in the back of the kombi, and roared away as we had come in a cloud of dust through the veld. We used our tub of well water till the city system returned to service, and then we forgot about it.

Some weeks later, reaction to this episode drifted back to us through our ministry contacts. They explained that a water well is highly valued property and is not shared except by permission. We had unknowingly stolen the water; the American missionaries were water thieves.

We sought out the owner of the well and humbly apologized. An African apology involves approaching the owner with head bowed and hands cupped together in self-effacement. Then a generous gift, such as food items, is offered as recompense. (Money alone would be seen as a crass attempt to buy out of the transgression.) I know we apologized but do not recall the exact details. However, it involved these elements along with words of penitence delivered by an interpreter who was authorized to embellish as needed.

Our training had stated there would be cultural differences, so we were on alert, but we'd still blow it from time to time as we did with the well incident. For example, another cultural adjustment occurred with the revelation that the women on our team were looked upon as less than virtuous when they wore slacks or pants in public. So the ladies ensured their public wardrobe consisted of dresses.

Americans, in general, are prone to cultural arrogance in a foreign country. It's been called the "ugly American" syndrome. The technical term is "ethnocentrism," which means you believe your home culture hung the moon. I had a revelation about this syndrome that I put in a letter home.

> *I've never had a great sense of national identity while growing up and I'm sure most Americans don't. We consider America the center of the world, kinda like "I'm American, isn't everybody?" But I've realized by looking at it from the outside that America for all its grandeur, is just a country and not a universe in itself.*

Ethnocentrism treats the local culture as inconsequential. Such an attitude would have fatally undermined our ministry. The apostle Paul identified the perspective of a true missionary: "I have become all things to all men so that by all possible means I might save some" (1 Corinthians 9:22).

We learned that to be effective working and ministering in Africa, one must become a student of the culture through observation and tactful questions. And through our occasional blunders, we also became students of contrition.

Anniversary

We passed the one-year anniversary of our arrival in Bophu on September 4, 1979, the halfway point of my two-year commitment.

By this point, the team had completed two LIFE evangelism training seminars and a third was scheduled for early the next year. We continued to promote the Here's Life campaign concept with the churches that participated in the LIFE seminars.

By our first anniversary, a number of local churches had become partners in our ministry, but not all. For example, I noted in my journal that a pastor we approached "respects us and appreciates us but apparently can't make use of us and is not willing to make our activities a priority to attend."

The faces in the small group that I led at Barolong High School had become consistent. I wrote home in October that we were working through Campus Crusade's *Basic Growth Series*. By mid-October, I had obtained approval from the school authority and started a new small group at Boitseanape trade school. At the end of November, both groups concluded for the holidays with the intent of restarting in the New Year.

Besides training and small groups, the team was sharing their faith in their everyday circle of contacts. For example, I talked about Jesus with crew foremen, the asphalt plant supervisor, and the magnetic board salesman. I shared Jesus with representatives from a long list of international companies: Firestone, Leyland, Toyota, and many others. My Tswana language tutor became a Jesus follower after I explained the good news of Jesus to him.

Extrapolating my numbers to the rest of the team, over two years, we approached several thousand Africans, black and white, with the claims of Christ resulting in several hundred life-changing decisions. However, it's essential to understand that these efforts were part of a wider goal to produce a self-sustaining ministry, that is, to equip Africans to save Africa.

Through small groups, seminars, meetings, and by personal example, many Tswana Jesus followers were taught and encouraged to share their faith with others and then to follow up with the new believers.

Our ministry efforts were intended to be lifted to a new level by the Here's Life campaign. I was spending a large amount of time preparing media and training materials in the belief that the community outreach would come about. But the campaign was still on life support.

It Will Not Go

In my September 1979 prayer letter, I wrote:

The responsibilities of my position with the government have multiplied several fold. It's a complex job but very challenging.

In my journal, I was more plainspoken.

As has been the case for quite some time, my job consumes most of my time and energy. Sometimes I feel very much alone; don't get much backing ...

Anything remotely mechanical might be thrown my way, from trivial to urgent. I was asked to assign a YB number to a push mower. I was given a letter to investigate the overflowing sewage system at a regional hospital. One morning I came into the office to find a genuine emergency: a failed pump at Disaneng Dam, a water supply reservoir. It took all morning to get the paperwork done and repair work started.

Another morning, Masibi delegated a call to me from President Mangope's office to adjust the temperature because his office was cold. I drove to the president's office at the parliament compound a few kilometers away. I passed through the security gate, and the solemn guards holding assault weapons, without being stopped. I entered the parliament building with only a piercing stare from the receptionist. I took the elevator to the president's floor and walked past his armed security guards into his office suite (the president was out). Alone in the president's conference room, I adjusted the air-conditioning thermostat and then left the way I had arrived.

Through all the layers of security, coming and going, no one so much as asked my name. I took away two lessons: First, the staff knew that "one of the Americans" had been summoned through lines of communication invisible to us. Second, we Americans could be identified without having to say a word. Perhaps it was something about the way we dressed or carried ourselves. So, in all likelihood, they knew who I was and why I was there.

My repair approval authority gave me purview over the heavy-equipment workshops. The workshop in Mafikeng handled the equipment in the western regions, and it was managed by the new seconded Afrikaans manager named Steve Le Roux.

Le Roux had worked many years in the nation of Botswana, which is adjacent to the northern border of South Africa, so he was accustomed to living under a black government and reporting to a black chain of command. Further, he had some proficiency with the Setswana language, a skill that was unique among whites. Steve Le Roux was a genuine, salt-of-the-earth fellow. He became a friend as well as a work partner.

Keeping equipment in good repair was a major problem. For example, we went through diesel engines like other shops went through oil filters. I wrote in a letter home:

We have a grader in the Kuruman area that has blown its engine for the 3rd time this year at a cost of $7-8000 per overhaul.

We received reports from the driver or operator when repairs in a workshop were required. The reports would be laughable, if not so sad. One report read, "The brakes operated wrongly and stopped the lorry and it will not go." In this case, the real problem turned out to be a seized engine that locked up the rear wheels. But the report was correct in that the truck most assuredly would "not go."

Another report explained that the damage to a bulldozer engine originated from a missing rain flap on the vertical exhaust pipe. When the equipment was parked for the night, the conscientious operator placed a rock on the pipe to keep rainfall from dripping into the engine. The report theorized that a bit of the rock fell down the exhaust, rolled into the engine, and the engine "packed up," or destroyed itself, when it was started. Logically, the exhaust system geometry should have made this explanation impossible. But logic and damage reports had a tenuous relationship, like old friends who weren't on speaking terms.

After reading these reports, it was clear the problems were originating from operator issues, like failure to maintain the oil level, fuel quality, or air intake. One of the white seconded officials theorized that many African youths lacked exposure to modern mechanical conveniences at home so they were not knowledgeable about maintenance. His theory had some truth: the chores of a black adolescent in the rural homelands would be walking behind the family sheep and goats rather than walking behind a lawnmower, or thatching the roof rather than tinkering with an automobile.

The sad fact behind the theory was that the lifestyle of blacks in the homelands was unlikely to change. Apartheid constrained the economic opportunities to acquire modern devices and the technical understanding to maintain them.

We made some headway on technical education by convincing our Toyota sales representative to provide truck-driver training. We organized the drivers into "schools" at each regional office, and Toyota truck dealerships sent qualified instructors. Facilitating this effort was a small but satisfying triumph.

However, like so many projects, it was a comedy of errors pulling it together. On the Monday that the first training course was to start, the Toyota trainer, a young white man, showed up at my office promptly at 8:00 a.m., but his hand was bandaged. He had an accident over the weekend and needed to go to a doctor. I sent him off for medical treatment and went over to the workshop to tell the foremen that the training would start late. But when I found the foremen, I learned that somehow, they had not heard about the training from the regional office.

At about 11:00 that morning, I went to the training room expecting empty chairs and was surprised to find that the trainer was back and setting up, and about twenty truck drivers were seated and patiently waiting for the course to begin. I gave an opening speech, using a translator, and it was off and running.

As a manager in Africa, it was never hard to discern a miracle.

Kruger

To celebrate one year in Africa, Joe, Mike, and I took a vacation to Kruger National Park. We packed the kombi with sleeping bags, clothes, and cameras and headed out on the ten-hour, 503-kilometer (313-mile) drive to Kruger, via a visit with Crusade friends in nearby Swaziland.

October 5

The high point of Sept. was going on leave with Mike and Joe to Swaziland and Kruger. The stress of work and ministry dropped away and I was free in my thoughts. Felt the closest to Mike and Joe that I have since we moved in together.

Kruger is one of the largest game reserves in all of Africa. In square miles, it's about the size of the states of Connecticut and Rhode Island combined. To the east is the international border with Mozambique, the former Portuguese colony, and to the north, the Limpopo River and the international border with Rhodesia (now Zimbabwe).

Paul Kruger, the president of an early Afrikaans republic, signed regulations in 1898 to protect the wildlife of the area. This was a few years before the British conquered his republic in the Boer War. The park region was not heavily settled by black or white because of the conservation effects of the mosquito and tsetse fly, whose presence "made vast areas of bush inhospitable to man, and thus provided the game with sanctuary from their most dangerous enemy."[1]

In 1979, it was permissible to tour the park by driving the hundreds of kilometers of unpaved roads in a personal car, as long as one didn't get out of the vehicle because it was quite possible to be eaten. At night, there were fenced camps with *rondavels*, round thatched-roof huts. Unlike rondavels in traditional villages, these rondavels came equipped with concrete floors, showers, cots, and a kitchenette. Camp conveniences notwithstanding, true wild Africa reigned within the park. Tent camping and on-foot activities were prohibited. Heavy fines were assessed if tourists were not inside the elephant-proof camp enclosures by nightfall. (Did I mention the potential for being eaten?)

The ambiance of our trip was provided by a cassette tape player in which we cycled our only Amy Grant music tape. It would play through one side, and we'd eject it, flip it over, and play the other side. When that side finished, we'd eject it and repeat. We all had a crush on the sweet spiritual songstress from Tennessee with the pretty brown hair. Along with the background music was the recurring click of single-lens reflex cameras as we found animals along the gravel roads.

The trip was idyllic—three unfettered guys, with days on our hands, plenty of film, and a park full of exotic animals in the wild. We photographed herds of stately kudu, graceful impala, and the odd wildebeest that had a head looking like "Beast" right out of the movie *Beauty and the Beast*. Herds of zebra in their prison uniforms grazed through the veld grass and a pack of frenetic hyena cubs chased each other in circles. A lioness in a dry riverbed stalked a giraffe and we waited, forever it seemed, for her to make her move (she didn't). From our vantage point on the bank, we could see both the crouching lion and the unsuspecting giraffe stretching its neck to forage among the treetops.

Speaking of giraffes, at times we were so close as to require leaning out the window backward and shooting straight up to catch a photograph. At a one-lane wooden bridge over a sluggish river, a crocodile waited patiently for a victim. Elephants, the true king of the jungle, meandered in herds through stream beds. They popped their trunks over the tall reeds like a periscope to sniff the breeze.

We stayed at several different camps including the exceptional Camp Olifant. It is built on a bluff overlooking the Olifant River with an expansive view east into Mozambique. September was the end of winter, the dry season. The vegetation on the plains of Mozambique was a dull gray-brown except at the river. Along the riverbanks, with their roots in the water, the trees, reeds, and foliage were a bright, life-affirming green. That memory is forever connected in my mind with the last verse of this passage:

> [1]Blessed is the man
>   who does not walk in the counsel of the wicked
> or stand in the way of sinners
>   or sit in the seat of mockers.

²But his delight is in the law of the LORD,
>   and on his law he meditates day and night.
³He is like a tree planted by streams of water,
>   which yields its fruit in season
> and whose leaf does not wither.
>   Whatever he does prospers. (Psalm 1:1-3)

The highlight of our safari was tracking two magnificent cheetahs padding through the veld grass parallel to the dirt road. Their golden coats with black flecks glowed in the dappled sunlight that peeked through the clouds. We were in a photo-shooting frenzy. The big cats obliged us by sitting upright on a fallen tree and facing us, no more than a stone's throw from the windows of our kombi. They seemed to be playing king and queen, seated on their thrones and surveying their realm.

I had a *déjà vu* impression watching these wild creatures: Could all this regal beauty happen by accident? By a chance mutation in some evolutionary phase? And what of all the colors, the intricate patterns, the strange shapes of Africa's gamut of animals—the trunk of the elephant, the neck of the giraffe, the horns of the wildebeest. Was this diversity required for survival of the fittest? If mere survival is the only criteria governing nature, why then did they not share the same traits instead of surviving so successfully while so riotously different?

No, none of this wild beauty was achieved by random accidents of nature. Nature is not merely utilitarian. It's diverse by design.

Author John Eldredge observes, "The sights and sounds, the aromas and sensations—the world is overflowing with beauty. God seems to be rather enamored with it."[2]

Eldredge further expounds, "The whole creation is unapologetically *wild*. God loves it that way."[3]

Africa offers a priceless gift to the world: a magnificent display of the Creator's love of extravagant beauty and his passion for the wild.

C. S. Lewis speaks of this wildness in his allegory depicting Christ as Aslan, a great lion.

> "Aslan is a lion—*the* Lion, the great Lion."
> "Ooh!" said Susan, "I'd thought he was a man. Is he—quite

safe? I shall feel rather nervous about meeting a lion." ...
"Safe?" said Mr. Beaver. ... "Who said anything about safe?
'Course he isn't safe. But he's good."[4]

Jesus is so good as to cuddle little children and bless them, so wild and unsafe as to challenge the governing elite of his nation and face death for it.

Chapter 18

THE HOPE

The old-fashioned drive-in theater, known as a bi-scope, located in a small town near Mafikeng, often showed American movies in English. This was a perfect destination for a group date. In an October 1979 tape recording, I reported that the drive-in was showing *Rocky II* and a quorum of the singles decided to give it a go. We threw in our lawn chairs and piled into the kombi. It was about a forty-five-minute drive on a paved highway.

Out from the lights of town, the veld at night was inky dark, like black cats in a coal bin. On one such night, a fire burned through the veld grass in the pitch-black distance. I noted the striking sight in my journal.

> *On the way home we saw a huge veld fire on the western horizon, at least a kilometer long. It stretched like an orange-yellow string on the horizon of the distant plains.*

No veld fire and little moonlight relieved this particular movie night; only the timid beams of the kombi's headlights pierced the dark. It was my turn at the wheel of the kombi. We hummed along the highway poking fun at each other, talking, laughing, and feeling very relaxed.

Suddenly, the veld all around us exploded in blue lights. I was blinded and stomped the brakes; the kombi skidded to a stop, and the engine died. We could then see a phalanx of well-armed South African policemen surrounding the kombi. The blue lights were from police vehicles just off the pavement. Officers flashed lights into the windows searching for we knew not what.

A young blond policeman approached the driver's side and shone a light in my window. We got acquainted in a friendly chat that went something like this:

Brash policeman, in Afrikaans, *"Wat doen julle hier die tyd van die nag?"* (What are you [y'all] doing here this time of night?)

Rattled American driver, in English, "I'm sorry, I don't speak English!"

I pause to point out that regardless of my overstimulated response to the policeman, I can speak English. (Read and write it too.)

Flustered policeman, switching to English and ignoring my incapacity in same, *"Auk nie!* Quite all right, no problem, carry on, carry on."

The policeman gestured with his flashlight for us to "carry on" and I did so as quickly as I could remember how to engage the clutch to restart the engine. He was so hasty to get rid of us that he didn't even check my driver's license. *Bless his heart.*

We weren't what the policemen were looking for, and certainly not what they were expecting. They may have been looking for anti-apartheid saboteurs crossing over the Botswana border, which was a dozen or so miles to the north.

My theory as to why the policeman urgently shooed us along is that when the officer realized from my accent that we were Americans, he feared some sort of international bad press. By this stage of apartheid, the South African government was sensitive to international pressure. It didn't need a newspaper story about harsh police tactics circulating in the US.

We made it to our movie, sat out in our lawn chairs under the stars, and watched Rocky Balboa win both in the boxing ring and in his romance with Adrian. The young ladies cried over the romance, and the guys all wanted to jog somewhere like macho Rocky. We loaded up and headed back to Montshiwa. On the drive home, the guys joked about needing to find a girl like Adrian.

The next morning, one of my sisters on the team approached me and said that the guys' comments the night before about "needing a girl" had been hurtful. We had been sitting among a car full of girls. What insensitive dorks we guys were that night. I apologized, and in the future had more respect for the feelings of the daughters of Eve that God had put in our midst.

This conversation begs a question: with all these eligible single people spending so much time around each other, were there no romances? Later. Be patient.

Rope for Hope

The Bophu government structure had three broad functions: executive, legislative, and judicial, which should be familiar to any American acquainted with high school civics. The names were different—for example, substitute "parliament" for congress—but the roles were much the same. Bophu inherited its structure from South Africa, which in turn inherited its structure from the United Kingdom.

Having the same structure, one might expect the Bophu government to function as well as its South African model. But it was not so; the narrow education and office experience of the average Tswana, because of apartheid restrictions, hampered the government's efficiency. I noted in a letter home that our principal problem at the department was a lack of qualified staff.

The typical civil servant was often uncertain what to do, so low-level decisions rolled up the chain of command, overworking those in management. This was why the performance of routine functions seemed confused and painfully slow. One of the enduring lessons I took from working for a government is that its effectiveness is not so much dependent on its organization chart as it is on the *capabilities* of the people filling its ranks.

Reporting to Secretary Masibi in the Department of Works was a deputy secretary and an open position for a principal engineer that managed the engineering section heads, which were something like department managers. I was, in effect, a section head, but I was unofficial: I had responsibility but not formal authority.

In this quasi-official role, I attended a four-hour budget meeting with the regional directors. I took some criticism related to priorities, but Mr. Masibi took up for me. Over the last few months, my standing had improved with Masibi.

I had a spiritual insight while sitting in this marathon meeting, which I related in a tape recording home:

> *"I was sitting in that meeting thinking God brought me here and has put me in this meeting. And so, you just have to trust him in those situations. I know he's doing things in my life thru all this stuff."*

Just like I experienced in June, my performance was directly challenged. But this time I believed God had a plan in "all this stuff." I had traded the end of my rope for the God of hope.

Vulnerable

In a November journal entry I noted:

> *[Since] I am the only mechanical engineer in the government ... I am involved with decisions for repairs that cost tens of thousands of dollars. The private firms which do these repairs are very competitive and I receive a lot of attention ...*

Even though my role was unofficial, I was called upon to make sizeable financial decisions. I interfaced with South African vendors plying the government for tender orders (awards of contracts), and these firms could be aggressive.

In November 1979, I solicited bids, analyzed offers, and recommended the award of a heavy-equipment order worth a half-million rand (about two million in today's dollars). In advance of this recommendation, the South African branch of a US heavy-equipment manufacturer invited me to tour their plant in Johannesburg.

I had a prospective workshop manager, Seretse, join me on the tour to deepen his understanding of heavy equipment. The company flew a twin-engine plane to Mafikeng to pick us up. In the four-seat passenger area, the two white salesmen sat facing Seretse and me with a narrow aisle running between us. It was cozy; our toes all but bumped. The white salesmen were personable, but it was awkward.

Seretse inadvertently added to the discomfiture. About halfway through the otherwise uneventful flight, he lost his breakfast on our nice polished shoes. Seretse, like most Tswana, had never had the opportunity to fly on a plane, and I hadn't figured on air sickness.

When we toured the manufacturing facility (after cleaning up), I noted that the assembly line alternated between road equipment and armored vehicles. South Africa in 1979 was under pressure from arms embargoes and unfriendly neighbors. Industry was engaged in national-security production reminiscent of the US during World War II. As its skills and capacity grew, South Africa became an international arms exporter.

I didn't realize it at the time, but I was in a vulnerable position. I was young, inexperienced, and a foreigner. Even more important, for the eight months after Mr. de Wet moved away, I had little in supervisory direction or oversight. It was by God's grace that I did not commit a vocational blunder. Management air cover was coming, but there was a major test first.

Light and the Dark Room

I was investigating leasing equipment to reduce our problems with maintenance and finding skilled operators. The Johannesburg-based sales representative for one of the many leasing companies called and asked to have dinner with me and the president of his company at the Mmabatho Sun, a local resort-quality restaurant. There were valid business reasons to get to know this potential vendor, so I agreed. We set the meeting for the next night and hung up. A few minutes later the salesman called back and said a lovely young lady in his office would like to meet me, and asked if he could bring her along. I said no; just he and the company president would be fine.

I arrived at the restaurant where I met the salesman, the company president (already inebriated), the company pilot (fortunately sober), and the aforementioned "lovely young lady"—the one I said could stay home. I recorded the details of the evening in my journal:

> *We proceeded to the dining room and the president, who was rather drunk, began peppering me with questions about my motivation (the girl seemed to always be at my elbow).*

The liquored president had been talking nonstop, but he must have realized he needed to engage the customer. He began to ask why I was in Bophu, and he was not satisfied with general answers about our mission.

> *At the dining room, we ordered and then in response to the persistent president, I asked the others if they would also like to know more of my motivation. They said yes so I passed The Four Spiritual Laws booklets around the table. On Law 3, they brought the food. I had mistakenly ordered a flambou [flambeau maybe?] steak. They fired up my steak by the table and then dimmed the lights so that everyone in the restaurant turned to look at our table just as I was sharing THE solution for man's sin.*

The timing of the "flambou" steak lighting was as if an angel decided to put an exclamation point on the "solution to man's sin"—that is, Jesus, the light of the world.

> *I kept going and explained Law 4 and what they needed to do to receive Christ. All were impressed but none committed.*

That no one wanted to make a personal commitment to Jesus was not surprising given the public setting. The president then launched into a discussion of his business; he had abruptly become sober.

We enjoyed a first-rate dinner (my flaming steak was perfect), had a solid business discussion, and established a good rapport. When I had heard all I needed, I thanked them for the evening and proceeded to excuse myself. The president protested and said I should stay as the night was young; simultaneously, under the table, I felt the young lady's hand squeeze my thigh. I stood up and with a *tot siens,* Afrikaans for "see ya," I headed for the door.

The salesman caught up with me and we walked to the entrance of the restaurant together. He apologized for the president's behavior and thanked me profusely for coming. I always wondered if his words were only to facilitate a sale. I had the impression, or at least the hope, that he also appreciated the light in what I shared.

The journal entry about that evening recorded this insight:

> *I saw a lot that nite. I saw how dangerous a man of principle is. When they realized I could not be bribed with booze or sex it changed the whole nature of the evening ...*

A New Boss

In November 1979, the department hired an engineer to fill the vacant principal engineer position. I analyzed my new boss in my journal:

> *Today, Mr. Franklin began work. First impression is that he's not the forceful take-charge man we need. But my job has made me more of a leader or at least brought out those traits, maybe it will with him.*

Mr. Franklin was a former municipal engineering director—he was an experienced, professional manager, originally from England, with a broad engineering background. My first impression was all wrong: Mr. Franklin would most assuredly "take charge." As far as being mild-mannered, he was, but he spoke with such a calm, matter-of-fact confidence, and with such faultless logic, that his leadership carried significant weight. I noted in a monthly journal entry that he was "helping relieve a lot of ambiguity from my job by defining the breadth and limits of my authority."

Although Mr. Franklin never joined any of our ministry activities, I always felt he was quietly sympathetic to our spiritual mission.

There is a little more in that November journal entry.

> *Writing the above [about the dinner and leadership] helps me see that God has used this job to develop my character and my leadership ability. I would never have known my capabilities without this job to stretch and test me.*

Chapter 19

THE DRAGON

In December 1979, the Bophu team traveled to Swaziland for the annual staff conference. Swaziland (now named Eswatini) was a beautiful little mountain kingdom. The land was folded into gentle, verdant hills, covered in a carpet of veld grass and mielie plots, on which traditional thatched roof rondavels and *kraals*, cattle pens, were clustered. In one valley, the US food brand Libby had pineapple farms. In other valleys, there were forests of eucalyptus and cedar trees imported from Europe.

Swaziland was bordered by South Africa on three sides—north, west, and south—and on the east by Mozambique. Like Botswana and Lesotho, Swaziland was a former British protectorate and had been granted independence in 1968.

The conference was held at the Luyengo Agricultural Training Center. Luyengo was a modern college facility built in part through donations from the Church of Scotland. We bought T-shirts proclaiming, "I Had a Good Time in Luyengo '79." Like the previous year, this staff conference was a rich spread of teaching, training, and updates.

Don Myers, Crusade's director for Africa, reported that revolutionary movements in many developing countries were challenging the spread of the gospel, but just as Jesus had taught, good was growing alongside evil. The church was seeing amazing results all over the globe. Crusade itself had seen tremendous growth in Swaziland: there were now ten Swazi nationals on staff with Crusade and some were ministering in other countries.

Myers also talked about risk-taking using Biblical examples of men that took risks based on their faith in God. He noted that when obstacles seem impossible, God works miracles. I reflected on the Montshiwa Here's Life campaign, which looked impossible. Our target was mid-February, but the churches were moving slowly. It all depended on God stirring up church members' hearts so that they wanted to do it; otherwise, there would be no campaign.

The Transcendent Culture

Reverend *Maswanganyi* (ma swan GONE yee), a writer and minister from the Shangaan tribe, spoke on culture and Christianity. His messages conveyed profound insights into the transcendent nature of the message of Jesus. He explained that the gospel is neutral to any national, ethnic, or tribal culture and therefore relevant to every man. The reverend stated, "The gospel is dynamic without Africanization or Westernization."

I made real-world observations of this concept in a letter home a few months later:

> *It is tremendously exciting to see someone grasp a spiritual concept and then share it with others in his own tongue. Pure Christianity is its own culture and when it is communicated that way, without western cultural trappings, it is very dynamic.*

Maswanganyi went on to say that all cultures, including European and African, have good and bad aspects. He encouraged us not to focus on changing culture: if the message of Jesus is embraced, the message itself will prompt any needed change.

Maswanganyi illustrated these concepts by highlighting a mistake that early foreign missionaries made. When mission workers began ministering in Africa, they taught Western culture alongside the message of Jesus—"the gospel of wearing pants." But Maswanganyi explained that it is "a great blunder for a missionary to try to culturize rather than to save." He was not condemning the missionary work; the missionaries brought Jesus to the continent and ultimately led to his own salvation. Maswanganyi's point was to encourage us to look at hearts and changed lives and not be distracted by cultural differences.

Maswanganyi also discussed the influence of the occult. Africans, even some who were nominal Christians, might be secretly consulting healers, shamans, or *sangomas*, popularly known as witch doctors. I never ran into any indication that the people we worked or ministered among were dependent on traditional religions, but I could have been deceived.

I observed a practice, particularly among young women, involving black bracelets, necklaces, and other loop jewelry that were worn to keep evil spirits from entering the body. This practice came across as a superstition, and yet I heard a story of a girl's conversion to Jesus and that it was a significant step of faith for her to remove her bracelets.

In another story of the occult, a newly married woman who was a Christian was forcibly taken to a witch doctor by her parents because she had not become pregnant. The witch doctor told her that she was not under any spell preventing pregnancy. Then he went on to say that the power in her, God's Holy Spirit, was greater than his own power.

Smitten

In addition to the Swazi national staff, Crusade had some fifty American expatriate staff in Swaziland; most were single Agape staff working as teachers or agricultural instructors. Mix in eight Bophu singles, over ten days, and the inevitable began to happen.

For me, it was a sweet, blue-eyed gal named Kathy. I was smitten. I tried to get her attention with some brilliant conversation but without effect. It was like she didn't even care about diesel engines. I'd learn sometime later that the problem was that my roommate, Joe, had picked out the same young lass, and he did get a positive response. Now how could Barney Fife expect to compete with Chuck Norris? It was an *"et tu Brute"* moment, as when Caesar discovered his best friend among his assassins. (That may be over-dramatizing a little bit.)

I was not so much hurt as embarrassed. I felt like I had been a very visible dummy, but I wonder if the object of my attention even noticed me (which may be worse than rejection). Joe and Kathy would have a cross-country relationship. I would have my Amy Grant tape.

Other romance stories were playing out at the time of which I was not aware. (I always seemed to be the last to know.) An American staffer flew 2,000 miles from the Crusade office in Kenya to join us on our post-conference vacation trip. Turned out he was smitten too, with my teammate Nancy. And later in the new year, an American staffer from Swaziland would visit Montshiwa to see my teammate Bonnie. Poor fellow, it would prove to be a wasted trip.

A Family Christmas

After the conference, the eight Bophu singles, plus Nancy's admirer, headed out in the kombi and the girls' Volkswagen Passat on a vacation trip to Cape Town. It's a twenty-five-hour drive from Swaziland, some 2,100 kilometers (1,300 miles), that crosses the southern edge of the African continent from east to west. The scenery of the drive is some of the most striking that South Africa has to offer.

Our route took us southwest through KwaZulu (the Zulu tribal homeland), across the rolling hills and farmland of the province of Natal. We passed through "traditional" areas with villages of rondavels, cattle kraals, and Zulu men on horseback.

At one stopping point, several ladies with painted faces, distinctive dresses, and elaborate necklaces were walking along the shoulder of the road. We wanted to take a picture of their costumes, for which they wanted money, and we refused. All for the best, as I observed later in a tape recording to my mom and dad, "They were bare-breasted so maybe it was inappropriate to take a photo." I was a master at understatement back then. In my defense, this was not an uncommon sight in rural areas of the tribal homelands.

On the Cape Town trip, I started a mustache under "Dakota Joe's" tutelage. His advice was to grow it long, because "you don't want a little Frenchie mustache." Whatever that was, I sure didn't want it. Mine would be as long and thick as I could squeeze out.

After passing through Natal and the Transkei homeland, the highway to Cape Town ran along the coast of the Indian Ocean. Some 300 kilometers (200 miles) of the highway is called the "Garden Route." The name comes from its lush forests and flora and from the many streams and rivers that cross the route on their way to the sea. To the inland side are the Tsitsikamma and Outeniqua mountain ranges, geologic children of South

Africa's Great Escarpment further north, in some places stretching out their craggy toes into the surf of the dark-blue Indian Ocean.

I have driven the gorgeous coastal highway of "Big Sur" in California, but in my humble opinion, the Garden Route surpasses it in drama, diversity, and sheer beauty. We camped out the next two nights in Tsitsikamma National Park and had some playtime on the rocky coast. The water was ice cold, but the sun was hot. I got a beet-red sunburn.

On Christmas Eve, we arrived at a little village by the sea: Herolds Bay. It was perched on a hillside that flowed down into a short crescent of sandy beach between two of those craggy mountain feet. It was similar to the quiet hamlets on the coast of Cornwall or Ireland's Wild Atlantic Way. The weather was even similar as it had turned cold and rainy. We settled for a couple of days in a quaint, family-run hotel to celebrate Jesus's birthday. By this point, we had left work and ministry concerns behind and were in perfect harmony with each other.

Ann had planned the entire trip including a Christmas party. We exchanged gifts and then took pictures of everyone "wearing" their gifts amid much laughter. On Christmas Day, the hotel prepared a Christmas feast much like we would have enjoyed at home. With all nine of us sitting around the table, it felt very much like a family. The companionship hushed the homesickness we otherwise would have felt. I was not focused on it then, but this was our last "family" Christmas together.

After Christmas, we made the five-hour drive to Cape Town. With expressways, skyscrapers, a diversity of ethnicities, and a modern seaport, Cape Town could pass for San Francisco.

Cape Town lies between Table Bay and the region's most prominent feature, Table Mountain, which at its summit has a flat plateau instead of a peak that looks like, well, a table. At 1,100 meters (3,600 feet), Table Mountain is like a giant version of a mesa from the US southwest. The wind flowing across the plateau can create a dramatic phenomenon consisting of white clouds that drape over the top of the mountain and down toward the city. It's called "Table Mountain wearing a tablecloth."

We became tourists for a few days. We visited the Castle of Good Hope, built by the Dutch in 1679, and the gorgeous Cape Town botanical gardens, which is where I learned what a protea flower is. We made a day trip south down the Cape Peninsula to the Cape of Good Hope, a rocky promontory that is generally considered the dividing point of the Indian and Atlantic oceans. Cape baboons cavorted in the parking lot.

Cape Town's history, culture, and beauty are a prize for any tourist. But for me, all this paled compared to the experience at the top of Table Mountain. We had been advised that the best time for a trip to the plateau of Table Mountain was shortly before sunset. We took the cable car to the top, and the expanse of the South Atlantic swept before us on two sides. A thin mist hung above the dark water, and directly in front of us, the sinking sun was beginning to settle into the mist. To the south, our left, the shadowy, jagged mountains of the Cape Peninsula were stained with gold from the fading light.

The wind picked up and wisps of clouds began to form and immediately flow over the edge of the plateau. Soon, a layer of clouds, the Table Mountain tablecloth, was flowing over the precipice on both our right and our left. It was as if we were standing on an island in the middle of a gigantic white waterfall. Meanwhile, the sun sank into the misty horizon in a blaze of yellow and orange that gradually ebbed away into the night. The stars that God had flung into the heavens above, and the lights of the city below flickering through the rushing clouds, took over the display.

Anticlimactically, we now had to get down the mountain. We huddled in cold, near gale-force winds at the cable car landing. I felt like a flag whipping around at the top of a flagpole. Finally, it was our turn to take the cable car down to the city.

What an evening! I wrote home that I never would have believed that I could have such sights and experiences. Jesus believed. He arranged it.

I came so they can have real and eternal life, more and better life than they ever dreamed of. (John 10:10, The Message)

How to Conquer Your Dragon

Our trip home to Montshiwa took two days of determined driving. The first piece of the trip took us northeast through the valleys of the South

African wine region. It's something like Provence, France. Miles of grape vineyards, ornamented with homesteads of Cape Dutch architecture, stretched away from the highway. But after a few hours, we began climbing the escarpment, and the mild coastal climate turned hot and dry.

South Africa has been described as an upside-down saucer, with the coastal areas giving way inland to the mountains of the saucer base, the Great Escarpment, and then the vast central plain. The eastern side of the central plain, where we lived in Bophu, is the high veld. The western side that we were traveling through is arid like west Texas: flat and rocky, tufts of scruffy grass, no trees, and few settlements. And it's big like Texas— it's called the Great Karoo. The Great Karoo's redeeming trait is sheep ranching, and, oh yeah, the odd diamond mine hither and yon.

Sadly, at the end of this perfect trip, after the wonderful fellowship and creation's beauty—after all that grace—I was in need of a character test. I wrote about the episode in my journal.

January 14, 1980 (Montshiwa)

Tonight at the team meeting we listened to a Ron Dunn cassette tape. God spoke to me thru it about something he's been saying to me ever since the trip to Cape Town.

On the trip during that final day in Cape Town when I was so mad at everyone and during the shame afterward, God spoke to me about just how ugly I was inside (the dragon from Lewis' Dawn Treader). I have not been conquered by Christ and therefore the anger was an outward thing I could not conquer ... that anger was so extreme and uncalled for it showed me how very bad off I was inside.

Without his conquest of my heart anything that I could do to change myself is a façade.

"For from within, out of men's hearts, come evil thoughts ..." (Mark 7:21).

January 28, 1980 (Montshiwa)

Today I wrestled with resentment toward others again, just like at the end of the trip when I felt like the "dragon." I guess the test is if I can stay loving even when I feel the opposite.

In his classic Narnia book series, C. S. Lewis writes of a spoiled, self-absorbed boy who, through his selfishness and greed, is turned into a dragon. It is a miserable, lonely experience, but the boy learns something important: being an ugly dragon reflected how he had behaved toward his crewmates on board their ship, the Dawn Treader. He wants to become a boy again, but the only way is for the great lion, Aslan, Lewis's allegory of Christ, to claw away the skin of the dragon. The boy described the process:

> The very first tear he made was so deep that I thought it had gone right into my heart. And when he began pulling the skin off, it hurt worse than anything I've ever felt. The only thing that made me able to bear it was just the pleasure of feeling the stuff peel off.[1]

What prompted my temper display that last day in Cape Town was a group decision that didn't go the way I wanted. Then I put into words the "evil thoughts" that welled up from within. In a note to John after this trip, I asked for prayer so "that I'll control my tongue better, I'm prone to be rash & unloving."

On the drive home from Cape Town, with my temper display fresh on my mind, the C. S. Lewis allegory lay heavy on my heart. I felt like the ugly dragon. The kombi was noisy at highway speed, and the driver and passenger in front had a bit of privacy from those in the back. On my turn to drive, Joe was in the passenger seat, and I quietly talked with him about how I felt. As always, he was accepting and affirming.

How many times will I have to humble myself and ask Aslan—that is, Jesus—to remove some ugly dragon skin? All I know is that to conquer and be free of the dragon, my heart must first be conquered by Jesus Christ.

> Above all else, guard your heart,
> for it is the wellspring of life. (Proverbs 4:23)

1980

GOD DOES BEST WHAT MEN CALL IMPOSSIBLE.
—SOURCE UNKNOWN

Chapter 20

THE FUTURE

We arrived safely in Montshiwa from Cape Town on New Year's Eve. After work on January 2, we went straight to the post office and, as we hoped, found a stack of Christmas cards and packages from home. Mom sent a care package of new clothes, food goodies, and socks (really, Mom?). Most prized were taco shells, which I shared, and some premium snacks, which I hid. One couple sent taffy from Gatlinburg, Tennessee, and cornbread mix—reminders that I was a Son of the South.

Another important item came in the mail a little later in January: my support report for December. I was relieved to see that contributions to my Crusade account had picked up in December after a decline in November. My contributors continued to be faithful.

The Promotion

Shortly after returning to work from the holidays, I began a series of discussions with Mr. Franklin, my boss, about the organization of engineering in the Department of Works. These discussions culminated in a meeting with Masibi, Franklin, three managers, and myself to finalize the appointment of four section heads. Mr. Pretorius would be responsible for roads and bridges, a newly hired civil engineer would be responsible for water and sewage projects, and a seconded electrical engineer would handle electrical projects. Finally, I was tapped, officially, to be the section head for mechanical projects and equipment.

This had been a long time coming. In one swoop, Franklin cleared away much of our organizational inefficiency, and a lot of my frustrations. I would be responsible for equipment procurement, administration, and the workshops. It was a big job, but not much more than what I was already doing. I had come a long way from spray paint and stencils.

For an entire year, since Mr. de Wet had taken me into his "section" the previous January, I had to use persuasion to get the job done, which forced me into a people-oriented leadership. I think God's purpose in keeping me waiting for this authority was to provide this seasoning. If I had not gone through a preparation period, if I had been dubbed "the man" at the outset, I would have been overconfident and overbearing. But Proverbs 15:33 counsels that "humility comes before honor."

Odds and Ends

January was notable in other areas ...

John and Lynn were expecting, and Lynn was beginning to show. Their child would be the second white baby born in Bophelong Hospital. John and Lynn would name their son "Pula," Setswana for rain or blessing.

Language learning had dropped down the priority list. Although I had mastered a substantial number of Setswana phrases using the LAMP methodology, it was difficult to connect phrases into a conversation. Regarding the Afrikaans language, I noted in a January journal entry that I attended a meeting in Afrikaans in which I followed much of the conversation.

The journal entry also highlighted a lunch conversation with a tool vendor. The conversation moved into spiritual topics, and I read through *The Four Spiritual Laws* with him. He said he was not a Jesus follower, and he might want to become one, but he explained, "I'll have to think about this. You see, I've never read the New Testament and I know nothing of Jesus because I'm a Jew."

The vendor talked through his religious upbringing, and I shared a few Bible verses about the Messiah. We both believed in the same origin of faith as recorded in the Old Testament. Although he did not make a commitment at that time, he now had the information he needed to become a Jesus follower.

Also in January, I wrote a letter home about my new leadership role at work.

> *We have a dam project going up with construction being done by the department. The engineering consulting firm says the workshop is not keeping the machines running. My workshop people say the construction people are abusing the equipment, who am I to believe? But for all that I enjoy responsibility and authority. The Lord provides grace for me under fire.*

The Future Shows Up

January 27

John and I had a meeting to discuss my future with Crusade. He wants me to extend a year and be the team's part-time administrator and then return for a second term and be administrator on a full-time basis.

Just as my official position at the Department of Works solidified, and with my impactful Here's Life role on the doorstep, the future showed up. My meeting with John was prompted by the coming fulfillment of our two-year government contracts at the end of September, some nine months away. John's proposal had two aspects: First, putting off furlough and extending a year, and then after taking furlough, returning for a second term to be the full-time administrator of the Bophu ministry. The administrator position would handle budgets and human resources and in general manage the office.

The term "full time" is used to designate ministry roles that are occupations—for example, the staff of a church, or John's role with Crusade as our team leader. To be the full-time administrator would mean leaving engineering. That would be a sharp change in my calling.

My original call was to work for Crusade overseas for only two years, but that was before I'd experienced the life-changing fellowship, challenges, and growth while serving in Bophu. God reveals life like unrolling a scroll. So, a re-think of my calling was in order.

I wrote a letter to my parents that evaluated my future with Crusade.

I love Crusade and I love being on staff. I enjoy and am challenged by my gov't job and in another year might be able to see more of my work bear fruit both at work and in discipleship.

On the negative side, there may be a limit as to how much I'll ever see accomplished vocationally & some of my disciples will be leaving school and moving away after this year.

I ended the letter home with a question that had been recommended for evaluating this type of decision.

Do you think the impact I will have for the Lord in government or business will be the equivalent of being associated with Crusade, or rather will it be better than the impact I will have with Crusade? I guess this last thing is the issue (we must all be sure our talents are reaping the most benefit)...

Providentially, I did not pursue an answer to this question. The wording merges good stewardship with God's calling and, in the process, changes calling into an optimization problem. The Bible teaches that God's ways are not our ways (Isaiah 55:8-9), which can include what we think is "better." For example, the apostle Paul on his second missionary journey thought that the better place of ministry would be the provinces of Asia or Bithynia, but instead, the Spirit sent him to Macedonia, a province of Greece (Acts 16:6-10). When Paul began preaching and teaching in Greece, the continent of Europe was opened to the good news of Jesus.

As I mulled John's proposal, it was logical to review my journal entries related to the future.

I often have a fascination with technical stuff or in administrative/organizational topics that have no attachment to spiritual things. I wonder about my ultimate position or job and find my desire in the secular. And then I wonder, should that really be? For a Christian who has a world vision to desire less than full-time work for Him?

> *I've been hung up with a guilt trip that being in business or secular work was a cop-out for not being in full-time work overseas. But technical/secular work is where my desires are...*

These journal entries kept revealing a desire for a technical role and a secular vocation. At the same time, these entries reveal that I wondered, *Isn't ministry the more noble calling?* In the broad sweep of my training, I had no direction on this issue, and I struggled with it.

I once told Joe that I didn't trust my desires because I had misused them in the past. And if you don't trust your desires, you are in a quandary because desires, interests, and motivations can be a marker on the path of God's leading. John Eldredge writes:

> But doesn't Christianity condemn desire—the Puritans and all that? Not at all. Quite the contrary. . . . Christianity recognizes that we have desire gone mad within us. But it does not seek to rectify the problem by killing desire; rather, it seeks the healing of desire, just as it seeks the healing of every other part of our human being.[1]

Desires tied to our delight in the Lord are the ones God will help us pursue because he gives them to us: "Delight yourself in the Lord and he will give you the desires of your heart" (Psalm 37:4).

Over the next few months, I needed to nail down that my desires were emanating from a delight in the Lord. Then, I could be certain that the things that delighted me also delighted God.

As it turned out, I needed to be confident in my decision to respond to challenges about my calling. What, you ask, everyone didn't go along with what you thought God wanted for your life? Oh yeah. What I needed was someone to act as a spiritual bulldozer to clear away doubts. Later, at just the right time, God connected me with that person.

Gifts Part I

In February, we started a teaching series to help us discern our individual spiritual gifts per the Biblical instruction contained in passages such as Romans 12:4-6:

> Just as each of us has one body with many members, and these members do not all have the same function, so in Christ we who are many form one body, and each member belongs to all the others. We have different gifts, according to the grace given us.

I journaled that the outcome of the teaching session left me confused.

> *Duane gave a lesson on spiritual gifts. It included a [self] test to show where your gifts are. I scored high in knowledge, wisdom, giving and discernment and low in areas I had recently figured I was strong in—leading, administration, and prophecy. This sort of upsets my nice plans to get an MBA [master of business administration degree] and be a success in business.*
>
> *...I do enjoy technical things. I do enjoy being in a position of management ... so it's not all clear.*

In this particular exercise, the object was to grade yourself on your spiritual gifts. Later in the year, the team performed the evaluation, which was much more insightful.

Rogues and Rules

During the time I worked in the Bophu government, despite the constant rub of an inexperienced government with aggressive profit-focused private companies, I never heard of any bribery. I was never offered or solicited for a monetary payoff (setting aside the Mmabatho Sun dinner), nor did I know of anyone else who was. I never even sensed corruption, except in one instance.

> *Work tough as usual. Salesman Leverett at ofc. today. He is quite distasteful—he even plays up to me by being "religious." It is hard to be even civil to him, much less loving, except for God's power.*

Leverett was the most assertive of the vendor representatives I dealt with. His simple but insolent demand was for me to specify in my tender documents that all tires supplied with any equipment ordered by the government should be his company's brand. Although it was a well-known and reputable brand, there were plenty of other well-known and suitable tire vendors. I had no reason to specify one over another. It made more sense to me that as long as it met our specifications, the equipment vendor could supply any brand of tire he wished and thereby keep competition open.

The salesman wore me out with calls and visits—all of which had the same demand, and for all of which I had the same reply: no special treatment. After four months of harassment with no change in my response, he was frustrated. In one final visit, he stood at the door of my office as he was leaving and shouted, "I'll kill you!" He was smiling as if it were a joke, but it was chilling. Sometime after that last meeting, I received a memo passed down from a high level in the government that all government tenders should specify the tires of the company represented by Leverett. He had won.

Obviously, the salesman went over my head, above Franklin and Masibi as well, because either of them would have simply sent the guy back to me. Why didn't the official who wrote the memo do the same? Unknown.

I never felt like any of the other questionable decisions I saw were made for covert material gain. Instead, they reflected an innocent misunderstanding of rules or procedures. For example, Mike and I heard of a case where Department of Works' lorries were used in a chief's funeral. But tribal chiefs and councils had an official status and received a government stipend, so the individuals involved probably considered this a variation of official business. Nobody gained materially; no hand with palm-up waited for cash.

Exasperation with the slow-moving bureaucracy might be blamed for the equipment trailer incident that I recorded in my journal.

> *Last year, a government employee authorized a company to build an R6,000 equipment hauling trailer. This order was verbal only, with no tenders, quotes, or official gov't order. It has now got to the point where the company is ready to take*

> *legal action if we do not buy the trailer. The company sent a chap over last week to talk it over—Franklin called his hand. He said the company should have known better than to build for a gov't agency without an order.*

I didn't see this incident as corruption, because the vendor was not shy about demanding payment from Franklin and me instead of the government employee that originated the order.

Bribery was not a way of life for citizens interfacing with the government. This was especially remarkable when compared to many other developing countries in this time period. Why was graft not a problem? It's an important question.

My opinion is that the rule of law was the foundation of the government civil service system inherited from the British, but it was held in place by civil servants who respected the standards of Christianity. Author Ernest Cole wrote about South Africa: "Thanks to one hundred and fifty years of zealous missionary work, seven Africans in every ten profess the Christian faith. Of the white citizens, 94 percent are Christian."[2]

The Dutch Reformed Church and the Dutch Reformed Mission Church stipulated conformity to moral rules. Likewise, the teaching of the other major denominations, Anglican, Methodist, Assembly of God, and others, inoculated their membership against corruption through their moral precepts. Any of these denominations would have considered bribery shameful. All of these churches were well attended at the time. It appeared to me that the moral code taught by the churches constrained bribery among both white and black officials even under the distorted political system of apartheid.

My first enduring lesson from working in government was that government effectiveness depends on the *capabilities* of its personnel, regardless of its structure. The second enduring lesson was that government effectiveness rests on the *character* of its personnel, which rests on their spirituality.

All Cylinders

I noted in a February journal entry:

> *Tonite was prayer nite. As we went around the room taking requests, I was struck by how much ministry stuff we have going on here! Persistence pays off ... we're seeing an impact for the Lord.*

After a year and a half of groundwork, the ministry was hitting on all cylinders. Soon, God would breathe life into that metaphor with a taxi and a cabbie named Elias.

Chapter 21

THE GIDEONS

John wrote about Here's Life in a team prayer letter: "Our role is simply a catalyst, and our strategy is to help churches become more effective in their ministry." We were here to encourage and provide training, but the churches had to own the Here's Life campaign.

Joe as prayer coordinator called us to fast and pray for the campaign every Monday as a team and then, individually, to pick a day of the week to pray. Prayer cells were organized at churches and in government offices. The prayer movement pushed through the spiritual inertia and opposition.

In a letter home in January, I noted that several churches had decided to participate. The relationships we had developed with pastors and church leaders, and the vision conferences to inform and inspire them, ultimately bore fruit.

By the beginning of the Here's Life campaign in March, one hundred church members had been trained through LIFE seminars in how to share their faith. Given the slow start, this was miraculous. The outcome can only be attributed to the prayer movement.

The trainees represented only a few of the local churches. One of the participating churches had only six members and the largest barely a hundred. We were truly like the Old Testament story of Gideon and his forty warriors taking on the hordes of Midianites.

In February, Here's Life coordinators from other countries came to Montshiwa to take notes on our preparations.

February 25

Team meeting tonight and as the coordinators conference starts tomorrow the conferees (2-Botswana, 3-Lesotho) attended. It was encouraging to hear from them and inspiring to have them with us.

Suspense

The Here's Life campaign had two phases. In the Suspense phase, posters, banners, and a sound truck were used to saturate the community with the slogan "I Found It!" In the Reveal phase one week later, the media message was changed to "I Found It, You Can Find It Too, New Life In Jesus Christ!" In the Reveal phase, the trained church members would staff strategically placed information centers and explain how interested people could find "new life in Jesus Christ."

The Suspense phase started on Thursday, March 13, 1980. We put up paste-board placards on every available public space that announced with cheerful blue lettering on a white background, *Ke Se Bone!* (kay say BOW knee), which was Setswana for "I Found It." We passed out hundreds of these placards to the church members trained for the campaign. They appeared on house walls, goat fences, store windows, street signs, and utility poles.

I wrote in my journal:

What a busy day, but fantastic. This morning I spent putting up posters in stadt [Montshiwa] shops with Magogwe, Phako and Makgetla [Botswana/Lesotho coordinators]—one of the greatest experiences I've ever had. People everywhere are asking, "What is Ke Se bone?"

Then we also had the sound truck driving through the neighborhoods continuously blasting out the campaign jingle: *"Ke Se Bone, Ke Se Bone, Ke Se Bone, KE SE BONE!"* I noted in a journal entry how the jingle was recorded:

Today perseverance paid off—I got a good jingle recording [for the Here's Life sound truck]! I got the copy of Swaziland's jingle, got a good tape recorder and tape from John and just started chasing all the leads to find someone to do the singing. Ended up at the Congregational church where Ann and Steve were having a meeting with the youth. With a bit of coaching, they did well.

The tune was simple and catchy, the voices were enthusiastic, and the recording was intelligible (more or less).

The sound truck was a passenger van with a loudspeaker on its roof held down with bungee cords. It was a taxicab when not recruited into evangelism, operated by Elias, a member of one of the participating churches. The sound-truck idea proved to be the most effective media method, particularly in the outlying villages where there were fewer places to hang posters or banners.

The taxi-turned-sound-truck was a sight to behold as it rumbled through the villages, jingle blaring, trailing a cloud of red dust, with a dozen or so barefoot, singing children running alongside.

Saturday, March 15

Today at the worker's prayer rally, I gave a talk on the Reveal phase and led a prayer time. Afterward as I went to the back of the room, Rev. Gumede [Crusade's regional director] gave me a pat on the back. Several times in these last few days, John's told me I'm doing "excellent." That's all been very encouraging—I have been working hard and long hours. But often these last few days, I've seen that the times I pushed myself might not have been necessary; God was working things out without need for me to stress myself out.

Rev. Gumede gave a strong talk today on the urgency of the hour. It indeed is. I saw in him how focused he is on ministry and I remember Frank Barker and how completely devoted he is. Must sack out, the brain is refusing to function.

The simple Ke Se Bone slogan left the entire town of Montshiwa and the surrounding villages talking about what was found and who found it. People wondered if it was a play or a show. I overheard one person comment, "Isn't it something to do with the Department of Health?" Another person asked, "Is it a new political party?"

In a March prayer letter, I related:

> *The owner of one of the scattered country stores in the outlying villages would not let me put a poster on his fence till he had my assurances that he could have whatever was offered for free. I chuckled inside as I thought of Ephesians 2:8-9 which says that salvation is the free gift of God.*

Where Had We Been?

After seven days of saturating the community with the "I Found It" slogan, we started the Reveal portion of the campaign. Beginning at 5:00 a.m. we glued an addendum to the bottom of the placards: *Botshelo jo boswa mo go Jesu Kereste. Ke jaaka le wena o ka bo bona,* meaning "New life in Jesus Christ. You can find it too." We also hoisted up new banners and changed the jingle on the sound truck.

It was then we learned that our translation of "I Found It" into Setswana—that is, *Ke Se Bone*—was not fully correct. Standalone, *Ke Se Bone* was fine, but when used in combination with the rest of the message it should have read *Ke Bo Bone.* How this nuance was missed with the many Tswana speakers involved with the campaign was a mystery.

This problem did not affect the balance of the Reveal slogan, which was correctly translated. So we forged ahead. I recorded in my journal:

> *Friday, March 21*
>
> *This should have been written yesterday [when the Reveal phase began] ... It was a long day, I started at 4:00 with prayer and then down to Duane & Steve's to make sure they got off all right to put up the reveal posers. I worked on a giant arrow banner to put up on Lucas Mangope Hiway [to point to an information center].*

At 8:00 a.m., with some predictable last-minute confusion, the church members opened the information centers. The sound-truck driver used a microphone to direct people to the centers. Throughout the day, Duane and I drove around ensuring all the placards had been marked with the "You Can Find It Too" message, replacing stolen placards, transporting workers, and restocking tracts at the booths.

> *Duane and I started driving to the info centers to see what was happening, the coordinators were with us. Met a discouraged Rev. Tobi at Montshiwa shopping center—none of his people were there. It was a cloudy cold morning and I prayed it wouldn't rain.*
>
> *Took Rev. Tobi to the bus rink [bus station] where Mrs. Shuping was with some of the congregation by the information center banner we'd put up the night before. These were all women but they were aggressively witnessing to the men. Left Tobi there. A lot of driving around as we get people moved to the shopping center. Ma Kagiso arrives and immediately begins witnessing.*
>
> *The situation at the bus rink is fantastic—everybody is sharing [how to find new life].*
>
> *It's now time to shift some people from the shopping center to Parliament gate for lunch. Rev. Ramosadi is very concerned that his workers (who are not employed and therefore have no money) don't have food. I want to slip him some money but keep my mouth shut as Duane is very solidly noncommittal and even indicates that the church should provide support for its workers.*
>
> *After this, we get organized and put the arrow and information center banners up. They look good but all the ropes look like a circus tent.*
>
> *It was really exciting to see it all come together and actually work. Over a hundred came to Christ on the first day.*

Of all the many moving parts, the surprise star was the sound-truck driver, Elias. I wrote in my journal:

> *Elias is a taxi driver and it is a sacrifice for him to drive slowly around the township with only the "I Found It" jingle and a loudspeaker rather than paying customers. However, by the time the "reveal" stage of the campaign began, he was working at it full-time besides spending time at the information centers witnessing. The sound truck turned out to be a key to the success of the campaign ...*

At mid-afternoon of the first day of Reveal, I had a conversation at the bus rink with Reverend Tobi and it summed up the campaign. It went something like this.

"Where have you been?" asked the good pastor, leaning into the driver's window of the kombi.

I looked into his dark leathery face and watery eyes and my mind wondered, *Where had we been?* Duane and I had been all over town.

"Where have you been?" he asked again, more intensely.

"Well," I began our defense, "we've moved people around, we picked up more booklets and posters, and then we went to ..."

"No, no, no," interrupted Reverend Tobi, shaking his salt-and-pepper head. "Where have you been all of the years we tried to get people to come to church, *when we should have been going out to them?*"

Reverend Tobi's face glowed with excitement. I looked behind him at the line of men and women standing in the dust of the passing traffic, waiting at the table to talk to a church worker about how they could find Jesus. I hugged Reverend Tobi through the window.

At the end of the day, I was dirty, tired, and still embarrassed about the mistake with the translation; after all, I was in charge of the materials. But it didn't matter. God does not want our perfection. He wants our faithfulness.

The information centers were overwhelmed from the first day they opened. In the first three days of Reveal, over six hundred people indicated decisions to receive Christ as their personal savior. The pastor of the six-member church led twenty people to Christ. The next day, he led a group of school children to Christ, one of whom was President Mangope's daughter. It was hard to determine the final statistics as many of the record books were unaccounted for, and many churches were witnessing outside the information centers. John estimated over a thousand decisions for Christ in the first two weeks.

The results of the campaign were due to Africans sharing their faith in Jesus with other Africans. The campaign participants, like Reverend Tobi, realized it was their calling to reach their community with the gospel. They had caught the vision.

The pastors and church members who participated continued to share the good news of Jesus with others long after the formal campaign concluded. For many, witnessing for Christ became a way of life. The churches organized follow-up Bibles studies for the new believers. At least one of the participating churches reported a dramatic increase in membership.

Like Gideon routing the Midianites, a group of small churches, armed with cardboard posters, canvas banners, and a taxicab, swept every dusty corner of their community with good news. The only thing extraordinary in this mix was faith in a carpenter named Jesus.

Afterglow

The church members, the pastors, the coordinators, and the American messengers experienced an afterglow as the campaign came to a close. The months of work and prayer had reaped a fulfilling and joyful conclusion. It was something like a Bophu sunset: the drama of the day was followed by beauty and calm.

> *Saturday, March 22*
>
> *Last nite we had the Coordinators over for dinner and tonite the team had a going away party for them at John and Lynn's. They have been a very special foursome and they have taught me a great deal.*
>
> *The last few days have been a blessing ... I felt like I was communicating with and understanding Africans—both our*

local pastors and the coordinators. It was great to be on the same plane with them and to have things in common, i.e. Here's Life, which we were both excited about.

But sleep calls—

The Montshiwa Here's Life Campaign provided a powerful lesson I will never forget. What feels like plain old hard work may be the ministry of Jesus working through us. Jesus himself labored, felt tired, and was dirty at times, but he worked anyway knowing God would use his efforts. I felt we had the exact same experience.

Chapter 22

THE PUZZLE

After the Here's Life campaign concluded, a government trip to Pretoria provided a pair of spiritual lessons.

> *March 26 (Pretoria)*
>
> *Went to see Mr. Maritz to pick up film for Alex (Mmabatho executive prayer breakfast Monday). He gave me some cassette tapes. One was Hendricks' "Knowing the Will of God." Heard again—God is no ogre, he wants us to be happy. If we like something that doesn't mean it isn't His will for us.*

God created happiness—Adam's fall in the Garden of Eden misdirected our search for it but did not destroy it. This thought would play into a conversation I was about to have regarding a future of secular work versus ministry.

> *March 27 (Rustenburg)*
>
> *Tomorrow I see de Wet with his usual knotty problems and strong personality . . . I'm thankful for it though, for what God has taught me and built into me thru it.*

In my Bible study notes on 1 Samuel 17, the story about Goliath, I wrote that Mr. de Wet was my biggest "giant." However, I also noted, "But God has arranged the whole situation." My interaction with de Wet was another opportunity for iron to sharpen iron, as described in Proverbs. My leadership was the better for it, but the deeper victory was that I recognized God's role in it.

Puzzles and Ping-Pong

In April of 1980, the fall in southern Africa, six of the Bophu singles decided to make a long weekend of the Easter holiday. We traveled to a beautiful area called Blyde River Canyon (now known as the Motlatse Canyon), located at the escarpment east of Johannesburg. Gorges, hills, and lookouts provided a sweeping view of the *laeveld*, the low-elevation veld beyond the escarpment.

> *April 4 (Graskop—Blyde River Canyon)*
>
> *We got in about 2:00 AM to the "Summit Lodge." Had to wake up the manager to get in, but they were very friendly and helpful.*
>
> *This trip I want to be the reverse of Cape Town. I want to, in God's power, put the needs of others over mine and be a servant.*

I spent time on this brief trip recording thoughts about my future. I had to solve this sacred versus secular puzzle. God spoke to me through certain Bible verses about this decision.

> *Factors Concerning Vocation/Ministry Call*
>
> *This has been a tough decision to sort out; it seems to get down to a conflict between two correct yet seemingly opposing facts.*
>
> *1. God has promised if we delight in Him, He will give us the desires of our hearts. I do sincerely want to do His will and my desires are in a secular field rather than Crusade.*
>
> *2. The battle is pressing & the laborers are few. Crusade is one of the best Christian outfits going and therefore one of the best ways to serve effectively in the battle.*

- *Deuteronomy 6:11-12, "then when you eat and are satisfied, be careful that you do not forget the LORD ..."*

  God seems to be saying if you are given the vocation you desire don't let it turn you from the Lord.

- *Psalm 32:8, "I will instruct you and teach you in the way you should go ..."*

  God will give the guidance I need, if I am not stubborn but trust him (32:9-10).

- *Ecclesiastes 3:13, "That everyone may eat and drink, and find satisfaction in all his toil—this is the gift of God."*

  It is good to enjoy one's work, but the finding of that satisfaction is up to God.

- *Joshua 22:3-4, "For a long time now—to this very day—you have not deserted your brothers but have carried out the mission the LORD your God gave you. Now that the LORD your God has given your brothers rest as he promised, return to your homes in the land that Moses the servant of the LORD gave you on the other side of the Jordan."*

  Not too sure on this one, it seems too obvious. But maybe God is saying my part in opening a ministry in a new country, as I put on my preference form back in AIT, is done. Now I must cling to what I've learned thru it.

The Joshua passage was a parallel to my call to ministry in Bophu. In ancient Israel, during its conquest of the promised land, two and a half of the twelve tribes of Israel were assigned land on the east side of the Jordan River. However, they joined with the rest of the nation to cross to the western side of the Jordan and help their brother tribes conquer the land. Once this campaign was completed, the eastern tribes recrossed the Jordan back to their land in the east and settled there.

Using the Joshua passage as an analogy, the Crusade ministry in Bophu was now established. Therefore, my role was completed and I could go back to my home in Alabama. As I had requested during training, I had helped establish a ministry where Crusade had never served before. The circle was complete.

April 5 (Graskop)

Had a long talk with Duane last nite, mostly about my future, during a ping pong game.

He gave me a lot of encouragement about going into secular work and having a ministry there. He talked about at least one man who decided against going into full-time Christian work because he felt God could use him more in his executive position.

Duane also talked a bit about how we should attempt to work at what our strengths are and at what we enjoy. Even though we often are not in that type of position and God still uses us, that should not be what we seek. This relates well to me becoming administrator of the Bophu team which is a job I don't think I'd enjoy.

Duane was, and is, one of the most faithful, God-honoring men I have ever known. In our pick-up game of Ping-Pong, Duane nailed it all down for me. Working in my strengths, and working in what I enjoyed, was what God wanted for me, even if this work was secular, not sacred. Duane acted as a spiritual bulldozer to level my doubts.

After seven straight days of prayer about my future, I'm at peace and have made the decision to keep my vocation in secular rather than full-time ministry. This nixes the Bophu administrator job and seems to make extension unwise. If I am being called to have an impact in the secular/business world then I need better experience than I can gain here.

Tentatively looks like the end of October to go home.

I wrote my folks to let them know I was called to secular work and would return to the US in September or October. I can imagine the relief and excitement that letter brought.

Regrets and Recoveries

I noted in a journal entry: "Not to close a door but don't feel up to two discipleship commitments." This may have been because my job at the Department of Works was often requiring more than forty hours a week and my role as media coordinator was also time-consuming. After the start of the New Year, I focused on developing the new small group at the trade school, instead of continuing with the established and eager group at the high school.

However, it proved difficult to meet with the trade school students. Five guys agreed to attend a LIFE training seminar, but only two came and they did not stay for the essential second day when we shared our faith in the local neighborhood. I focused a lot of attention on one particular student, but I had a hard time scheduling meetings with him. I carried a regret home from Africa that I did not try hard enough with these guys, but my journal entries indicate they were just not that interested.

Looking back, the choice of small groups was not wise. An enduring lesson with such a decision in ministry is to follow where the work of the Spirit is evident.

Small group discipleship had been an emphasis of our training. Because of this small group breakdown, I felt for a long time that I didn't complete my mission. But God had a broad ministry for me in Africa. Witnessing at work, leading training, and the "I Found It" campaign were all part of this wider work. These areas were also emphasized in our training.

In addition, many ordinary labors were foundations for ministry such as flogging a tape recorder into obedience, being a good neighbor in a Tswana community, and organizing a fleet of equipment that resembled the debris field of a hurricane. God brought all these diverse pieces together to form a ministry. And he did this individually for each one of us on the Bophu team.

At a higher level, a focus on *personal* ministry was a narrow view of my calling. I was called to Africa as part of a *team*. My particular gifts and abilities were most effective when used with my teammates. Jesus followers are members of a body and are called to make individual contributions to its life as a *whole*.

For example, I had forgotten about the discipleship group that I co-led with Mike at our government office. The work of the Spirit was obvious in this small group. The numbers varied from week to week, but four of the young men were mentioned regularly in my journals. Mike and I took them into the community to share their faith, which they were eager to do, and had them over to our house for meals and social times.

One of the four, Isaiah, was a clerk who worked in my section at the Department of Works, so I was his supervisor as well as his small-group leader. We had something of a mentoring relationship. I noted in my journal:

> *Isaiah, my helper at work who prayed to receive Christ with me earlier in April, has been very faithful about coming to the study ... It turns out he's Dutch Reformed so he comes to my church...*
>
> *Isaiah is developing into a genuine disciple. Since we work together there's plenty of exposure to each other. I had prayed and set a goal back in A.I.T. to have one chap brought to a level of maturity before I left. Perhaps God has provided that individual.*

In writing this memoir, I discovered that regrets I carried for years were not necessary and that prayers were answered in ways I did not recognize. Despite mistakes and all too often dragonesque behavior, my calling was fulfilled. This is the work of God: he accomplishes things hoped for and reveals things not seen. To his glory and praise.

Jesus, Meet Apartheid

Most Africans did not own cars, so we were frequently asked for a lift here or there. These courtesies became ministry opportunities or cultural education, or both.

THE PUZZLE

May 10

I had a trip to Pretoria/Ga-Rankuwa on Thursday & Friday.

Some guy wanted a ride to Mafikeng from Ga-Rankuwa and I very reluctantly agreed. He read thru The Four Spiritual Laws and with a little explanation (Rev 3:20 means saying "tsena" [enter] to Jesus) he prayed to receive Christ. We sang songs, listened to Ron Dunn [cassette tape recording], etc. He kept saying it was a "fine journey" cause we talked about Jesus. It was indeed.

A few days later I recorded two thought-provoking cultural experiences.

South African Notes:

1. Tues. afternoon drove to Lehurutshe to look at site of new Stores Depot. Took a representative from [the Department of] Agriculture. A Tswana, older man who had been in gov't service since leaving school in 1950, a few gray hairs, stubble mustache, dignified quiet air, clean but mismatched grayish suit with red sweater vest. He was sort of aloof at first, but spoke such good English I wondered if he would just chuckle at my Setswana. Very courteous, though quiet, wondered if there could possibly be any racial antagonisms stored away or if he just accepted it all.

Shared how to become a Jesus follower with him and feel very sure he was a Christian. This opened him up and he became very friendly.

Heard me speaking Tswana to a chap at the depot and he really was delighted. On the way home we had a Setswana lesson ...

Also, on the way home he made this statement, "Is there another country in the world that oppresses people like South Africa. Withholding the good for themselves ..."

Most of the good, arable land of South Africa was not found within the tribal homelands. As a research group noted, "In fact, there is a close and probably not coincidental association between the northern and western edges of the Republic's maize [corn] belt and the southern and eastern bounds of Bophuthatswana."[1]

I'm not sure this is what my passenger was referring to when he said "withholding the good for themselves," but being in the Department of Agriculture, he was probably aware of the disparity in the quality of farmland between South Africa and Bophu. Underneath his calm, reserved demeanor he was seething from either the land differences, or other injustices, or both. I noted in my journal that I was amazed at the contrast between my first impressions of this fellow and what was going on inside him.

From my experience with this gentleman, I was reminded that we can never assume that emotions are not there because they are not on display. In a cross-cultural conversation, the emotional cues may be different or repressed.

Later he [my Department of Agriculture passenger] talked about African culture. He said that if the word "communist" was derived from the word common, then Africans were the first communists because they hold everything in common. Little ones grew up sharing. There were no fences, none of the "this is mine" of Western culture.

The fact that my passenger brought up communism reflected the worldwide conflict in the 1970s between Western democracies and communism that sometimes played out in African countries. Reverend Maswanganyi, who spoke on culture at our staff conference, provided some clarity to my passenger's line of thought. He stated, "The sense of sharing of Africans is not from Marxism, it is indigenous African."

Africans' understanding of communism was complicated by apartheid. South Africa had laws aimed at suppressing communism that were frequently applied broadly to any opposition to the state. A boycott or labor strike, for example, could trigger severe penalties. Under these oppressive laws, Africans might see validity in the expression "the enemy of my enemy is my friend."

2. Wednesday morning went to the bank with Ann. Ann was in line at her bank [I was at a different bank] and at the end of the counter, at a window for special transactions, a black woman suddenly passed out and fell down. Nobody moved. A few blacks gathered around but they didn't know what to do. Ann went to help and did some first aid like raising her feet. No whites came to help. The blacks said give her water (Ann said no as the lady was unconscious) and one wanted to put water on her neck.

One fellow came up and started with Tswana greetings and small talk with Ann, "I go to the same church as you." The absurdity was surreal. Eventually, the teller that normally waits on Ann came over and asked what was the matter. Ann asked her to get an ambulance and one did come.

Ann made the remark, "Life is so cheap. The people did not consider this woman's life worth losing their place in line."

I don't have a good way to explain this incident, much less redeem it. I know both blacks and whites would offer help to strangers in need. I think this was a case of everyone expecting someone else to make the first move. The white tellers probably expected the blacks to take care of their own. The Tswana were probably afraid to take initiative in a white-run establishment and were inhibited by their lack of first-aid skills.

Whatever the combination of reasons, the result was an example of compassion stifled by the apart-ness of apartheid.

The Future II

Finally, I got back with John about his proposal that I return for a second term and be the team administrator. I recorded in my journal that:

I talked with John about my future this afternoon. Told him I didn't really think God was calling me into the administrator post. He again said he wanted me to extend so that the ministry wouldn't fold up from people going on furlough all at once. I said I'd pray about it and my loyalty to the ministry makes me want to help out in this way. The thought of missing another Christmas though tears at my heart; lately I've been more homesick and missed America more than ever before.

Soon after talking to John, the Department of Works began to ask what was up with our plans.

May 19

Today at the engineer's Monday meeting, Franklin pressed me and Mike for our future plans. I told him I had preferenced an October departure date with no plans for a second term. I don't think he was surprised, but I did sense it was sort of a blow to him to finally have it out. He didn't try any persuasion otherwise; I suppose I sounded very definite. He did mention if we were to plan to come back, things would reorganize as to broaden our experience. I don't know if that would be possible for me. With my thinking as it is now, I would not accept it in any case.

Owners of horses know the animals tend to start speeding up, even galloping, as the rider turns the reins back to the barn. It's called barn sour. The barn represents food, shelter, and companionship of the herd, and when a horse sees the barn up ahead, it is anxious to get there. As the time to departure got short, I was turning barn sour. I was anxious for home.

The first of October, and home, were four months away.

Chapter 23

THE YOKE

> IF YOU ARE FILLED WITH PRIDE, THEN YOU WILL HAVE NO ROOM FOR WISDOM.
>
> —AFRICAN PROVERB

Jesus preached to a crowd of followers in Galilee:

> Take my yoke upon you and learn from me, for I am gentle and humble in heart, and you will find rest for your souls. (Matthew 11:29)

The word yoke brings up a mental picture of oxen wearing a heavy wooden crossbeam interlocked with a wooden necklace. But when you think of a human wearing a yoke, the picture switches to medieval peasants, prisoners of war, or some other scene of brutality. And yet ... Jesus says we should willingly put on his yoke and we will have not torture, but rest. How can that be?

Let's admit that the thought of wearing a yoke is revolting. It involves control by someone else, not ourselves—not a popular thought for a society that worships personal freedom. And so, we resist the yoke of Jesus.

Discovering my "yoke" was preceded by difficult experiences. But through the humbling of those difficult circumstances, I accepted Jesus's yoke. Eighteenth-century commentator Matthew Henry writes:

> But in coming to Him they must take His yoke, and submit to His authority.…It requires self-denial, and exposes [one] to difficulties, but this is abundantly repaid, even in this world, by inward peace and joy.[1]

There is an easily skipped over phrase in Matthew 11:29: "Learn from me." When I arrived in Africa, I needed to learn from Jesus, which I could not do without submitting to his yoke. Wearing his yoke, I learned how to live more peaceably toward others, and in that new spirit, I could be fulfilled and successful using my spiritual gift.

About his yoke, Jesus said, "For my yoke is easy and my burden is light" (Matthew 11:30). Pick any task or activity you gladly anticipate and enjoy doing. Whatever burden of work is involved is light because of the joy the task or activity provides. The yoke of Jesus rests easy and the burden is light because of the deep satisfaction and fulfillment in life it brings.

We do not need to fear wearing the yoke of Jesus. When Jesus says, "My yoke is easy," the word "easy" in Greek, *chrestos*, can also mean "well-fitting." Yokes of wood are custom cut to fit the ox—tailor-made, so to speak—so that they do not injure the animal. Commentator William Barclay writes:

> So Jesus says, "My yoke fits well." What He says is: "The life I give you to live is not a burden to gall you; your task, your life, is made to measure to fit you."[2]

Remember my experience as a dragon? The well-fitting yoke of a Jesus follower will never fit over a heart bloated with the dragon skin of pride, selfishness, and self-sufficiency. When my dragon skin was torn away, through sometimes painful experiences, only then could I wear the yoke that Jesus made for me. If there is one essential enabler to find the yoke that is easy and to carry the burden that is light, it is this: *a humbled heart*.

The Scroll Unrolls

In my initial call into missions, I was prompted by an intersection of need, ability, and desire, which was then confirmed as a calling by wise counsel and my commitment to act. In addition, circumstances verified my call: the Crusade screening process, the training checkpoints, and the provision of financial support. A final confirming circumstance was my mother's illness and her full recovery complete with her unquenchable grin.

The elements of calling changed when the direction of travel was reversed. Need, ability, circumstances, and commitment were not much of a question in deciding to leave staff and re-enter the marketplace. Instead, my desires drove my decision as validated by counsel and specific scriptures. A key scriptural confirmation of my call was by analogy with a passage in the Old Testament book of Joshua. It said to me that since I came to help start a new ministry, which was now in place, my role was complete.

The chief concern was that I wanted to work in a secular setting versus a ministry context and I was concerned about this "non-spiritual" desire.

Pastor David Guzik observed that "full-time" ministry occupations (pastoring, for example) are not the only ways to advance the kingdom. He said, "God forbid that we should buy into that kind of thinking. Wherever God has placed you there is a kingdom calling within it."[3]

The apostle Paul wrote a Bible passage directed at workers who were Jesus followers:

> Whatever you do, work at it with all your heart, as working for the Lord, not for men. (Colossians 3:23)

The word "whatever" is written without exceptions or limitations. It is all-encompassing: plumbers, teachers, and engineers as well as pastors, missionaries, and choir directors. ALL things, secular or sacred, are to be done as if working for the Lord rather than human masters. All Jesus followers are *equally* working for the Lord in whatever endeavor to which he leads us. In that sense, all vocations are sacred.

The discussion with my teammate Duane helped me see that my desire to be in a secular vocation was from a heavenly father who loves me. Jesus said, "If you, then, though you are evil, know how to give good gifts to your children, how much more will your Father in heaven give good gifts to those who ask him!" (Matthew 7:11). Therefore, the desire could be trusted.

Another affirming passage is from the Psalms:

> Praise the LORD, O my soul,
> and forget not all his benefits ...
> who satisfies your desires with good things. (Psalm 103:2, 5)

God is not an "ogre." He loves us. If I was sincerely seeking him, I could have confidence that the desire to be in a secular, not sacred, vocation was compatible with a call from God.

Finally, just as I had counselors who expressed concerns about me *entering* the ministry, I also had counselors who had concerns about me *leaving* the ministry. I weighed the criticisms and considered their validity as I had in my first calling, but I was more careful with warnings the second time around. I didn't shrug off any input. After prayerful consideration, my sense was that the opposing views were calibrations, but not stop signs.

The two calls, initially to go and later to return, had a common point that was indispensable: finding a call comes through prayer—that is, a sincere asking, seeking, and knocking.

The Uniqueness of a Call

During my term of service in Africa, I had two questions that evolved from a misplaced understanding of calling:

Was I "more spiritual" (committed, dedicated, faithful) than those at home who did not go into ministry? This question puzzled me.

Conversely, was I "less spiritual" (committed, dedicated, faithful) than my teammates who stayed in full-time ministry? This question haunted me.

But I have come to an answer for both questions.

God creates us uniquely in the womb. He gives us different personalities, abilities, strengths and weaknesses, spiritual gifts, circumstances, and opportunities, just as he gives us different fingerprints. Devotional writers Amanda Jenkins, Kristen Hendricks, and Dallas Jenkins remark:

> Read His word and you'll discover that He created you, formed you, redeemed you, and called you by name. He'll

tell you He has a plan for your life and that you're not a discount, sort-of-close-but-not-quite version of anyone else. You are you, and you have a specific purpose.[4]

If we are truly asking, seeking, and knocking, then the only explanation for our different directions in life is that each Jesus follower is on a path designed specifically for him or her.

Each member of my team in Africa had a unique call: a personal reason they were called to Bophu. It was particularly obvious to me with my roommate Mike. Mike identified with Africans in a way that I could not. In return, Africans sought Mike out; they confided in him and befriended him. I would meet people in town and they would say, "Oh hi, Bill, where's Mike?"

God gave Mike the ability to build deep relationships with Africans, and ultimately, with internationals from all over the world. With this special gifting came a special call: Mike spent his working life in ministry with the majority of his career located in Africa. He and his wife from the southwest US were married in Africa and raised their children there. I greatly admire Mike and his call and commitment.

I believe that I was called to be a short-term missionary, an engineer, and a man of business. And now I am called to write this book.

Finding a calling can be difficult country to tread through; each Jesus follower must hear the Master's voice for himself. We must each seek and knock and call out for wisdom, and then we must trust it when it arrives. This is not easy, but consider: God has our every hair numbered. We believe in an all-knowing and all-loving God. We can trust Him to tell us, every unique child of God among us, how we are to spend the rest of our days on earth.

Chapter 24

THE CRUCIBLE

I once observed a military helicopter flying north over Montshiwa, perhaps to patrol the Botswana border. In remote Bophu, this was about all we saw of military activity. I wrote my mother that we knew of only two sabotage incidents since our arrival, as if any non-zero number would have assuaged her fears. The government was not releasing information about all the violence that was occurring across the country and over the borders, so my number was probably low. During our tenure, the South African military, police, and other security agencies were very busy.

I have always connected my memory of the flyover with the June 1980 attack by ANC saboteurs on the SASOL coal-to-oil refineries—an event we read about in the newspaper. The bombing's physical damage was substantial, but the impact on South Africa of a successful assault on such a key installation was even greater psychologically, which was the ANC's true objective. The ANC's military wing, *Umkhonto we Sizwe*, "Spear of the Nation," was established in 1961 by Nelson Mandela. After Mandela and other ANC leaders were imprisoned, the ANC operated from the party's headquarters in exile in Zambia and was directed by Oliver Tambo, Mandela's former law firm partner.

The ANC had been using the tactics of peaceful resistance and negotiation since its founding in 1912 and was influenced by the non-violent principles that Mahatma Gandhi used successfully in India. But after fifty years with no improvement in the rights of blacks, and with the introduction of apartheid, which further deteriorated their freedoms, the ANC changed its tactics to include violence.

Mandela and Tambo were unlikely military leaders. Forty-something lawyers when the military campaign was initiated, they were office workers and city dwellers who knew nothing about weapons or warfare. I doubt in their upbringing they so much as lit a firecracker.

At the inception of the sabotage campaign, intentionally injuring persons was expressly forbidden by the ANC leadership.[1] The ANC leadership judged that black-on-white bloodshed would alienate the white population from any future multiracial society and government. But even if unintended, the ANC attacks resulted in collateral injuries and death to black and white civilians, such as when the South African Air Force headquarters was bombed in 1983.

The ANC learned how to wage a guerrilla war, but South African security forces were proficient at countering infiltration and sabotage. It was ultimately economic pressure that forced white political leaders to begin negotiations with black opposition leaders. This pressure came from the cumulative effect of the cost of defense and security, a fall in the price of gold, dwindling capital and growing debt, and trade restrictions.

The first meeting between a South African government delegation and ANC leaders occurred in 1987. After seven years of negotiations, these talks led to free elections and in 1994 Nelson Mandela became the first black president of the Republic of South Africa.

Gifts Part II

Duane concluded his teaching series on spiritual gifts in June. The lesson included an evaluation through which we identified each other's spiritual gift(s). This was an invaluable opportunity to have brothers and sisters, who had observed one another closely for two years, to make an informed and loving judgment on our individual gifts. In my journal I noted:

> *Duane finished his series on spiritual gifts by giving a test in which everyone [my teammates] had a chance to mark which gift they thought everyone else had. I scored high in governments (administration), giving, and prophecy, and no others.*

In my notes from Duane's teaching, I scribbled that a Jesus follower with the spiritual gift of "governments" will "organize and manage, make things go smoothly." The team's evaluation that this was one of my spiritual gifts probably reflected their observation of my Here's Life role as media coordinator and my role managing the government's equipment fleet. Duane noted in his teaching that a person will gravitate toward those things he enjoys and is successful doing. Indeed, I had found that organizing and managing was satisfying work.

In my time in Bophu, my spiritual gift and my occupation as a manager were aligned, but that may not always be the case. The apostle Paul had a skill, tent making, that he used, at times, to support himself financially. It was separate from his calling of teaching and preaching.

The teaching on the gift of governments also noted a key requirement: "Are you able to endure reaction to yourself personally in order to get the job done?" *Auk nie mon*, do we have to talk about that problem?

God had been working on my ugly tendency to react to others ever since I'd landed in Africa. My ability to align my work with my spiritual gift, the area where I was satisfied and could be successful, depended on my spiritual growth in an area of weakness: being loving, patient, and forgiving. I had to be less full of myself and, crucially, more full of Jesus.

I called our offices in the Imperial Reserve "the crucible," meaning it was a place that God used to remove spiritual impurities.

June 20

I had been feeling that I'd grown in the area of patience and wise "impossible" responses. But as Ron Dunn says, when you think you're strong, you've become very vulnerable to a fall. In the last few days, I've been acting unloving and unwise and had a few bad scenes with Botha and Makgabo ... pretty foolish of me.

The Imperial Reserve crucible did its work in finding an impurity; I wasn't strong in patience and wisdom. But the point not mentioned here is that "I" never would be. Jesus said, "Apart from me you can do nothing" (John 15:5). The secret of the Spirit-filled life is to let God live *through* us.

As C. S. Lewis writes, it's not our brilliance (strength, patience, wisdom) that we are to reveal to the world, but God's:

> It is easy to acknowledge, but almost impossible to realize for long, that we are mirrors whose brightness, if we are bright, is wholly derived from the sun that shines upon us.[2]

The Programme

The Department of Works' Mafikeng workshop was only about a block or so from my office in the Imperial Reserve. I walked over once a day, or as needed, to see how things were going and have a cup of tea with the workshop manager, Steve Le Roux. He sometimes had a memo or maintenance bulletin for me to read and we had a standing joke about whether I could drink and *dink*, Afrikaans for think, at the same time. He also showed me the day's catch of quirky repairs in the work bays adjoining his office.

In June 1980, I came up with a plan that I surely bounced off Le Roux in one of these visits to his office. The equipment suppliers had workshops for their brand of equipment located in different cities close to various regions of Bophu. The concept was to redistribute the Bophu fleet of equipment on a brand of supplier basis so that the machines were close to their respective supplier's workshop. For example, Caterpillar had a workshop near Kuruman, so why not locate our Cat equipment near Kuruman? Service obtained from the Cat dealership's workshop would be much closer than returning machines to the government's workshop or traveling to Kuruman from Mafikeng to provide service.

This would lower the burden on the government workshops, decrease response time and travel costs, and thereby increase the availability of the equipment to do its work. Further, the department was going to issue a tender soon for new heavy equipment. The government practice was to award the entire order to the lowest bidder. If the cost difference could be justified, what about ordering from different vendors and locating the new equipment near the respective suppliers' workshops?

The idea was simultaneously logical and radical. It was outsourcing some of our maintenance needs to non-government vendors, but our equipment availability was so poor that it was time, I thought, to throw in the towel and do something different. I referred to this scheme as the Procurement and Standardization *Programme* (program). The idea began to get some traction around the Imperial Reserve.

We continued to attempt to automate the inventory of heavy equipment using the Department of Finance's mainframe computer. The first trial run of a report occurred in May, but by mid-June, I noted in my journal that the computer system was "bogged down," whatever that meant. In hindsight, it's remarkable the homeland had any electronic systems at all.

Home Folks

To get us through to the end, God decided to send the "USO" again. As had happened the previous year, an American singing group toured through our boondock town. This time it was the Logos Singers from LaGrange College, Georgia, located only twenty-six miles from my home in Roanoke, Alabama. It was so close that I had friends who lived at home in Roanoke and went to college there. These singers were "home folks," as we would say in the South, located a veritable stone's throw from my family. We got to know them after their performance at a friend's house.

> *June 24 (letter home)*
>
> *As we sat in a friend's living room Sunday nite, I could have been sitting in Roanoke. All the accents were right, I understood the jokes, we talked about places I knew. It's weird 'cause I experienced joy and trauma at the same time. Excitement over being back in a familiar culture, yet a nervousness 'cause you're not sure you fit-in.*

Of all the college singing groups in the United States, God had sent home folks. I needed this additional prod from home because the last dozen weeks presented difficult challenges to my decision to leave Africa.

> *Still wound-up and disturbed inside after the time with Logos
> ... It must be something like re-entry shock. Sudden re-exposure
> to your home culture. Just like they predicted at AIT, I've
> become a 3rd culture somewhere between home and here.*
>
> *Today, Mike got the telegram saying his grandmother had died.
> I was with him when he opened it . . . Rough day.*

At the team meeting in late June 1980, John passed out a training manual, *A Guide to Reentry*. In their inimitable manner, Crusade trained us how to undergo the emotional stress of returning to our home culture. As with all of our training, the manual was incisive and practical. It told us to get ready for a bumpy ride. We would be leaving what had become familiar in Africa to rejoin what had once been familiar, but would now feel foreign, at home. From the manual:

> Suddenly, we find ourselves out of phase with our own culture. Reaction comes in the form of bewilderment, dismay, disillusionment and perhaps even irritation or anger. Somehow, "things are just not the way they used to be," "nobody seems to care," "nobody really understands."[3]

It was like culture stress in reverse. My reaction to the visit of the singing group was a foretaste.

Crusade's international support staff's penchant for organization, their conscientiousness with detail, and their absolute devotion to our cause ensured that we field staff were prepared for almost everything we encountered. During our AIT training, someone in a cubicle somewhere faithfully graded our tests, read our weekly reports, reviewed our AIT journals, gave us encouraging notes, and monitored our progress to ensure we could be a success. They checked-off on our vaccinations, made our travel arrangements, and were there for us if we had a mishap.

Now, at the end of the term, they provided preparation for re-entry. They would meet with us soon after we returned for a debrief, and then provide whatever help they could offer for our next calling. Only now, with years of organizational experience behind me, can I look over the breadth of the process and fully appreciate what was done to make us as effective as possible in the country God had called us to serve.

Changes

June 8 (letter home)

Finalized the equipment buying program for this year. Among other things we'll be buying 8 graders, 2 loaders, 14 dump trucks, 9 water trucks, 1 tracked and 1 rubber tyred excavator, and about 12 tractors: total cost 1,9 million rand [about $10 million in today's dollars]. I've planned which old equipment will be written off and where the new stuff will go.

In a long letter to the Bophu tender (procurement) board, I had requested that the department's new heavy equipment be bought on a different basis than low bid. I had drawn up a detailed analysis of the savings in equipment downtime from locating equipment near supplier workshops. My motivation came back approved without comment. (I experienced a harder time getting the magnetic board approved!) I think they were blown away by all the numbers and decided to trust the American engineer and his British supervisor. Unfortunately, the new equipment would arrive after my departure and I would not see my grand programme put into practice.

Meanwhile, I was also coordinating with the road crews, regional directors, and workshops to relocate the existing fleet as much as possible near its respective supplier workshops. The response was mixed; personnel were suspicious about such a sweeping change but admitted it would help. I could never have attempted this without the good relationships I enjoyed.

June 29

I've let it become common knowledge at work, for better or worse, that I planned to leave between October and December. Worry about my departure date; would rather stay longer to see that new equipment is properly allocated but I don't want to go home alone.

July 7

Today, we had an Engineers meeting and Franklin pressed Mike & me for details on our plans. Later, Masibi called me into his office and wanted to know, demanded to know, what were my plans. Told him I wanted to pursue my career in my home country which is the truth but may not have been tactful. He was really distressed (as was Franklin earlier) which made me feel like I had been useful. Told him again how honored I've been to work in his chain of command. He responded by saying it's been good having me.

One year ago, my work had warranted disapproval from Masibi; now, my work warranted serious concerns about my departure.

The ministry chain-of-command was altered in June. John asked me to report to Alex and assist him with the Executive Ministry—an outreach to senior government officials. John was overdue for relief from overseeing thirteen staff, a wide span of control for any supervisor.

Further, Alex was due some help in an initiative that he had developed largely on his own. The outreach to executives had an impact at the highest levels of the Bophu government. For example, Alex had a road trip to Pretoria with the top executive of a government department with whom he worked closely on development projects. Alex explained how to become a Jesus follower to him and the executive asked Jesus to come into his life.

I wrote home:

Please be in prayer for our work and the men involved in the Executive ministry. We had a discussion group two weeks ago with 2 cabinet members. One of them, the No. 3 man in the government, is unbelievably on-fire for the Lord.

In August, Mr. Franklin and I discussed the operation of the engineering organization. I wrote in my journal that he requested I prepare "a proposal for a new chain of command for the engineering branch" before I left the country.

So many of the valuable ministry and work projects that happened in the last half of my term in Africa were locked out in the first half by my self-interest and self-defense. Wearing the well-fitting yoke of Jesus freed me to contribute to God and man. Another paradox of walking with Jesus is that only as we submit to him do we become truly free.

Saving Eternity

Wednesday, July 9

Steve Le Roux had a very bad pain in his chest yesterday and went home. The Dr. said it wasn't his heart and that he needed to see a specialist (internist). Went to see him at lunch today. Had talked to [wife] Joey over the phone and she said he and also [their daughter] were worried he would die. When I got there she said it again. I shared John 3:16 and said that I know my eternity was safe because of my relationship with Christ. Then I asked if I could share The Four Spiritual Laws, they assented. Asked Joey to sit on one side Steve on the other & went thru the book. They prayed to ask Jesus into their hearts!

This was one of the most meaningful experiences of my time in Africa. I loved this family. We met every Sunday night for the remainder of my term to watch the news on TV and then study the Bible.

Sunday nite, July 13

Back to the Le Roux's tonight. Took my Bible and we had a follow-up appointment ... Talked for a while and watched the news, then off with the TV and they pulled out their Bibles. We went over assurance of salvation particularly 1 John 5:11-13. Joey said Steve has been morbid lately talking about death; maybe this will help. They were very keen to listen; had questions; relaxed & good time!

Becoming friends with the Le Roux family provided anecdotes of Africa.

Later, Steve talked about the Kalahari bushmen & gave me a picture of same. Wild that he knew these strange people so well.

Said they'd live in short huts until the particular bok [deer] they'd shot [with poisoned arrows] was all gone, then move on to the next waterhole. He used to hand out food on his [heavy equipment repair] trips as part of a gov't relief program.

Also, Joey talked some about when identity documents were first issued in the late fifties (she was living in the Cape). To classify a person by race, they would check everyone's ancestors to see if there was a "crack" and the person had a black, Malay, etc. in his family tree. She said many who were living as Europeans, whites, committed suicide (one bloke drove his car into the sea) when a crack was found, thus making them Coloured. Reminded me of the Nazis.

News announced death of Botswana's Sir Seretse Khama. Steve said, "Botswana is finished."

Steve also talked to me about staying or coming back arguing I could be a big wheel, "a big wicket." Tempting, but I doubt it would be that great. And all I have to do is think of the forested hills of Alabama to renew my longing for home.

Return of the Dragon

July 18

The trip home has led me to some inner hurt and conflict. Joe and I had at one time talked of taking the trip back together. But then his sister [Mary] wanted to meet him on the way and he decided to travel back with her. It looked like it would be OK 'cause Mike then said he and I could travel together. But he kept reducing the time for traveling…

I've let these things and other imagined wrongs sap my walk and nursed hurt feelings, particularly against Joe. He came in last nite, really being vulnerable, to ask what was wrong but I couldn't tell him.

I had walled off my friendship with Joe due to some ridiculous hurt feelings. I was in my little bedroom reading when Joe stuck his head in. The conversation went something like this.

"You seem quiet, just wanted to see if there is anything between us?" asked Joe.

"No, everything's fine," I lied.

"You sure?"

"Yeah."

Joe knew I was not being honest, and he backed out of the room and reclosed the door. I said to myself, *Well that will do it, he'll withdraw now like I have and our friendship will be over.*

But the next day, Joe was as friendly and cheerful as ever, performing all the helpful courtesies roommates should do for each other: "Can I get that for ya?" "Here's your mail." "My turn to cook tonight, what're you hungry for?"

I was stunned: Joe reacted to my hatefulness by returning love. After a couple of days, I asked Joe for forgiveness, once again tearing off the ugly dragon skin. My roommates Joe and Mike never failed to return grace for my self-centeredness. In their own way, they demonstrated the grace Jesus offers to the world.

Now Wait a Minute

Hold on now—regarding the petulant conduct with Joe, hadn't I grown beyond such "dragon" behavior? And what about the emotional reaction to the college singing group from home? In July, I wrote in my journal:

> *Have begun to have inner turbulence about all the changes coming up. It will be painful.*
>
> *Things are moving quickly. I'm getting that sense of the end approaching and a sort of excitement and tenseness ...*

In a July letter home, I wrote that I gave my re-assignment preference form to John indicating I would be leaving Crusade staff. "John and I had already discussed it," I wrote, "but this made it official. It was emotional; neither of us knew what to say ... leaving is painful in a lot of ways."

Could all the competing emotions of departure—
> the tug of home, and the tug of a place I'd grown to love,
> the anticipation of seeing family, and the sadness of separation from my team family,
> the feeling of current job satisfaction, and the fear of starting over in my career,
> the simple anxiety of staring in the headlights of change—
> *could all of that be knocking me off-center?*

Maybe. In Crusade's re-entry manual was a timeline of emotional response while adjusting to, and returning from, a foreign culture. In the months "Prior to Return," expatriates experience re-entry stress even before leaving the host country. This stress could have several effects, such as lowering productivity and decreasing interest in the current assignment. Basically, these effects are a weakened ability to stay the course. In Alabama, that would be convincing proof of turning barn sour.

I would like to be able to blame my dragon behavior on something, even turning barn sour. And I would also like a reason why I became romantically involved in my last two months in Africa.

Chapter 25

THE WHIRLWIND

August 2

Just got back from dinner with Beth, Amy and Doris. Great evening. Had a good time joking around, then a good dinner, some games and a slide show. After the slides, Beth pulled out a book by an Afrikaans author (Bosman) of short stories. Very funny and tremendous insight into life and culture of the "boers."

Of course, there was a lot of eye contact and glances with Amy. I could get into a relationship if I wasn't careful. But I know our different nationalities are too much of a burden for anything serious and that's why I have avoided it. I do not want to lead her to think something is there.

Beth, Doris, and Amy were a few of the white South Africans working for the Bophu government to advance racial reconciliation. They were fascinating to be around. Their accents and choice of words were so engaging, and their manners so polite, that they were almost whimsical. Once I made tea and was told it was "lovely." They had been living not far from us and had been friends with the team for nearly a year.

The next day I added a follow-up entry to my journal:

I was really tense all afternoon. Part of it was from the inability to finish my "announcement" prayer letter which will give my future plans. Also, really wound up from last nite. I am infatuated and don't know how to handle it. All my careful "objective" reasoning seems a light burden to toss overboard.

Why would I even think about a romantic relationship with a South African now, at the end of my term, especially when I had been avoiding it? My only excuse is that the re-entry stress of my impending departure had unplugged my reasoning, and through that loss, the ability to stay the course.

Not Just Business

August 3

Good time with Le Roux's tonite; Steve's health is much better. We didn't do the lesson 'cause they talked and I got there late. They have fond memories of their time living in Botswana. Joey mentioned she had done her [Bible study] homework!

These Bible studies with the Le Roux family were wonderful times. Steve and Joey were so genuine, humble, and spiritually hungry. I felt if I had only come to help this one family, then it could have all been worthwhile.

August 11

Today, Dikeledi [Department of Works colleague] came into our office at work, sat on Mike's table and asked me ("the one who is leaving forever") if I thought my work in Africa was finished. I said that I know the work will go on without me. She said America has so many Christians able to help others grow and Africa has so few. Why should I leave? Mike defended me and explained that America had problems, that God is the one that calls here, there, or wherever, and also that I could go home to recruit. She was not satisfied but finally said ok & left. I was humbled.

Of all the appeals to my decision to leave, this was the most intense. I was taken by surprise and left without words. My roommate Mike, with whom I shared an Imperial Reserve office, had to answer for me, which he did adeptly and gracefully.

My decision on my future had been for the most part based on objective analysis. My conversations with Franklin and Masibi were along the lines of "it's just business." But Dikeledi confronted me from the heart. *Was she right, Lord?*

After more thought and prayer, I was not led to think my direction should change. But Dikeledi's words added a new level of chest-tightening angst to my preparations to depart. In an August 17 letter home, I wrote, "I dread leaving with the split up of the team and all the goodbyes and 'Are you coming back' questions. I am feeling a lot of stress and tension …"

It's Complicated

Crusade provided a three-month furlough for staff returning to the US from overseas assignments. Furlough was a time of rest and re-engagement with home culture, friends, and family. It was also used to re-connect with supporters. I planned to take the three-month furlough for speaking engagements, family time, and thanking supporters, and then I would re-start my stateside engineering career.

Five of the singles would be leaving Bophu for furlough on the same day. Crusade had booked a KLM flight on September 30 from Johannesburg via Nairobi to Amsterdam. After sight-seeing in Europe and England, I would fly from London to Atlanta.

But there were other moving parts in my travel plans.

> *Played tennis with Amy yesterday. She invited me to visit her home in Durban on my last weekend in South Africa. Said she'd show me the town, her mom would cook, explore beautiful Natal, catch flight Tuesday to Joburg to catch the KLM flight to Nairobi. I'd love to go. But I'm afraid of what I'm getting into. Afraid she might be hurt or even me too. I'd find my will and reason very weak with a pretty girl on a moonlit beach.*

I was in a quandary on whether to accept the invitation; my love of travel made it appealing, but fear of the consequences made me cautious. I discussed the relationship with my teammate Steve, and I realized through our talk that I must leave Africa with "no strings and with no hope in her that I won't fulfill." I was sensible, at that particular moment, and my will was under my mind's control, not that of my emotions.

I had lunch with Amy the next day and told her these conditions. I was proud of myself and felt that, with that said, I could go to her home in Durban. Then I promptly asked her out for Saturday night. There were contradictions and pitfalls in these decisions, but I didn't see them.

Tonite, date with Amy; went to the Taj restaurant to watch TV. She talked the whole time. Learned all about her prestigious family ... By the time the nite was over I was quite out of it; really felt inferior. Distressed that my American heritage seems so simple.

I learned that Amy and I had lots of differences. She preferred liberal arts instead of mathematics and science. We were attracted to different theologies and styles of church worship. Also, she held Afrikaans culture in low esteem, but said of English culture, "It goes back to Chaucer!" My ancestors on both sides were farmers, so I could identify with the pioneer spirit of the Afrikaners, though not their oppressive politics, and I loved the Le Roux family. Amy was attached to her upbringing and ancestry. If nothing else, this discussion validated that our backgrounds and preferences were radically different. I'd had relationships sink over less than this.

On her own initiative, Amy later apologized for slighting Afrikaners and technology and explained that what she treasured most in life were her friends, not her ancestors. So that ship was righted. I was impressed and charmed.

I moved past all our differences, like walking past a sleeping lion.

The Pretty Little Bakke

Wednesday nite, August 20 (Pretoria—Brookhouse)
On spur of the moment, joined Mike on a trip to Pretoria.

Went to Ga-Rankuwa and presented the procurement and standardization programmes and though much flak, I think it came across OK. Tomorrow we go back via de Wet's office and I'm sure there will be resistance there. I haven't kept up my relationship with de Wet which was always weak at best.

It was an interesting twist to our work assignments that some of the equipment the workshops maintained were used by Mike's crews to upgrade dirt roads into bitumen-paved roads. So, improving equipment availability directly facilitated Mike's work. For part of our term, we conveniently shared an office and one of those precious, high-tech devices: a rotary-dial telephone.

Large firms could throw around a lot of money to try and get our business, but there were also small enterprising companies. A proprietor of one such company visited my office and when I had to divert briefly to attend to a crisis, he took a seat and pulled out a book.

"What are you reading?" I asked.

He replied, "I'm working on my certification as a fire protection engineer."

I was impressed with his determination to catch any time he could to improve himself.

Steve Le Roux called me to the workshop one day to talk to a representative from a small parts-supply company. Arriving at the office, I knew he was working independently because his attractive *bakke* (BUH key), a small pickup truck, which was parked right outside the office door, did not carry the usual decals or markings of a company, indicating it was his personal vehicle. He was sitting in the office by the workshop manager's desk looking morose. As it turns out, we could not buy parts from him because Bophu used the South African government's annual parts tender, which had been awarded to one of the large Johannesburg companies.

I was repeating Le Roux's explanation and adding my regrets when, with the deafening roar of a wide-open diesel engine, a large tractor burst out of a workshop bay in reverse and at top speed. A wide-eyed Tswana wearing the blue coveralls of a mechanic was sitting at the steering wheel, but his shouting and wild gestures indicated he had no idea how to drive a tractor. Frantically looking over his shoulder, he suddenly pulled the steering wheel sharply to the right. The tractor made a tight U-turn and a beeline toward the workshop office.

The large rear tires struck square into the side of the pretty little bakke. The thick lobes of the churning tires all but climbed over the bakke, crushing the sheet metal of the side and door as workshop personnel struggled to get close enough to turn it off. Those of us inside watched in shock and retreated further into the office.

It was over in a few seconds, and the poor salesman collapsed into a chair with his head in his hands. I attempted apologies but he did not respond. I have rarely felt as sorry for a member of Adam's race.

Postscript

August 24

Played tennis in Mafikeng with Joe, Ann, Mike, Nancy and Amy. We matched up in couples (Amy & I together of course). It was a great afternoon; I played fairly well—Amy and I won a few games though not a match. Amy really has me charmed. She's going to make leaving extremely hard.

September 4

Relationship with Amy has really grown since last entry. I see her every day now ...

Given my previous recognition of our differences, there should have been red lights coming on in my relationship with Amy, but I had pulled my brain out of the circuit. The warning lights were dead.

The entries in my journal noted that my planning decisions were becoming jumbled due to this relationship.

Talked to John at his request on Friday about a P.S. he got on a letter from Don Myers. Myers remarked he was disappointed in my decision to leave staff and wondered if I've counted the cost to the ministry, to my supporters and in evangelism/ discipleship.

At the time of our talk, I was still in turmoil over the status of relationship with Amy so I was all mixed up with my future too. Couldn't answer John's queries on what I wanted to do. Did say I'd pray some more at a prayer retreat today. I still feel, after seeking God again on it, that engineering is where he wants me right now. So, I'll have to tell John & carry on. If God wants otherwise I trust Him to show me.

As Agape staff, we had two chains of command, one through our government positions—in my case up to Secretary Masibi—and the other with Crusade through the continental office in Nairobi to the continental director, Don Myers. With this note from Don, the symmetry was complete: both chains had asked me to reconsider. My ability to stick to my decision despite these challenges was another confirmation of my call.

Another romance was blooming on our team. One night my roommates and I took the kombi into town to eat out, probably at the Taj restaurant to watch TV. Ahead of us was a small blue car that looked like Duane and Steve's Ford. When it bumped over the hump of the railroad crossing of the tracks that ran to Botswana, the kombi's feeble headlights illuminated the inside of the car.

"That's Duane and Bonnie," I observed. I knew them so well I could identify them from the backs of their heads. "Wonder where they're headed?" I asked no one in particular.

Some murmuring came from my roommates to which I responded, "What, they're on a date?" I was shocked. I'd grown so accustomed to my teammates being brothers and sisters, and nothing more, that this was inconceivable.

Obviously, Duane wasn't near so limited in his imagination.

The Doctor's Diagnosis

September 7

Today I was convicted, while praying, about the need to talk with Amy about looking at things realistically. So I did talk,

I told her I'd been in a long distance relationship before and we had drifted apart despite copious letters and an occasional visit.

So where am I? Getting deeply tied up in a relationship that will soon be frustrated.

The long-distance relationship I mentioned above was my first love, which was interrupted by my family's move from Nashville to Memphis. If two hundred miles could kill a relationship, how about eight thousand?

Later in that last month, I told Amy that I didn't know how I would feel after all the adjustments at home and that we should be free to see other people. However, Amy brushed off this discussion, and no wonder: No matter what I said verbally, my actions were sending a different message. I was with her every free moment.

If my internal relationship warnings were not working, there were also external warnings. Crusade had policies concerning staff members dating non-staff. I was convicted enough to re-read my manual and realized I was sidestepping these rules. Joe felt the need to challenge and warn me about the time I was spending with Amy. One of my teammates met with me privately and speculated on whether we were in love. I noted that resolving the future of the relationship had become an "agony."

Many cubbyholes are used to simplify and categorize relationships. The obvious slot for this one is "whirlwind romance." But when you are involved in such a romance, it doesn't feel like a whirlwind; it feels like time has stood still as you are captivated by feelings and emotions. When so captivated, the will and motivation to act cannot get a toehold. However, God will lead a relationship where it needs to be, if we truly seek him.

September 16

Told God I want peace from him, regardless of how the relationship works out.

Dr. Henry Brandt owned a nationwide restaurant chain, was a consultant with General Motors for many years, and was now associated with Crusade to conduct marriage and leadership seminars and counsel Crusade staff members. Dr. Brandt held a PhD, but his teaching was not theoretical. He transferred practical lessons from years of life experiences in a compelling balance of wisdom, humility, and confidence. He stayed with our team for several days in mid-September giving talks to local groups and counseling individually with several of my teammates.

His visit was God-sent.

After one of his seminars, I arranged to accompany Dr. Brandt to his hotel. On the way, we had a two-line conversation that went something like this:

"Dr. Brandt, what is the meaning of infatuation?"

"Bill, it means there is an attraction with no foundation to build upon."

The most profound answer is often the simplest.

September 24

I see clearly now that my feelings toward Amy are infatuation in the sense, as Brandt put it, that there's an attraction with no foundation to build on. We're far apart on crucial issues: spiritual maturity, doctrine, politics, habits, expectations of husband/wife roles, and our upbringings were much different. I want to minimize these things but I can't and be honest before the Lord.

With the prompting of Dr. Brandt's wise counsel, I put my brain back into the circuit of my reasoning and red warning lights came on regarding this relationship. I saw clearly that critical hurdles existed that could not be resolved. I realized that retaining any belief that the relationship should continue was not in either of our best interests.

So today I had another hard-nosed talk about our future. It was the same content as the time before but I had determination now—I'm not going to let my actions betray my words ...

It was tough on both of us—we talked for a long time. Had seriously considered backing out of the Durban trip, but decided to keep my promise.

And with that determination, visiting Amy's home in Durban on my last weekend in Africa seemed very unwise. It would send confusing mixed signals on the relationship. In addition, I needed the time to finalize loose ends and attend to goodbyes. I wrote in my journal that I realized now it was a "B" decision. But my promise was still hanging out there.

September 26

On the way home I met Amy and Beth, Amy got in the kombi for a talk. She said simply but perfectly that she had thought thru what I'd said, and felt that the trip to Durban was not the way to end our time together. She said she knew that she had initiated the trip and was now ready to see me not go if I felt that was better.

I love the way God works in his children. God had steered Amy's heart and mind to a decision that ensured our time together ended with grace.

God's timing was exquisite: I had four days left in Africa.

Chapter 26

THE TEARS

Saturday morning, September 27

Rainy morning and cold. We haven't seen the sun in several days—strange weather for Bophu. Never thought my last days in this dusty place would be so soggy.

We didn't have a last Bophu sunset. Instead, being sad to see the sojourners go, Africa shed tears on the veld.

I got my huge California suitcase down from the top of my wardrobe closet and dusted it off (literally), along with a smaller bag for our time in Europe. Despite all the chaos in making plans, it ended up that Joe and his sister Mary, together with Mike, Steve, Ann, and I, would have a week in Europe together.

We would take the overnight train from Mafikeng to Johannesburg and its international airport. On the next day, September 30, we would board the flight to Nairobi. After a short stay in Kenya, we would fly to Amsterdam. Amy would take the train with us to Johannesburg to catch a flight to her home in Durban.

September 27 cont'd

Piet came by in the morning and accepted our counter offer of R3,000 for the kombi. Later that morning he had the check already; said we could use the kombi till we left. Everything we

> wanted & more. I must never forget the Lord is willing and able to provide more than we ask or think if we'll wait on Him and His ways to do it.
>
> Settled up everything with Mike and Joe on house and kombi— we're now "divorced." Gosh how these guys have blessed me ...

A footnote on God's provision: In US dollars, we paid $4,400 for the kombi. After twenty-three months, with current exchange rates, we sold it for $4,000. Our version of the African Queen cost us a net of $400, or, on a monthly basis, a bit over five dollars each. God gave us that wonderful vehicle practically for free.

> September 28 (letter home)
>
> Last nite we had a Braai [cookout] with all the team and retold all our funny stories & laughed and laughed ...

We attended the Dutch Reformed Mission Church one last time and I recorded the service with its enchanting music. I enjoyed one last Sunday night TV news and Bible study with the Le Roux family. I had a final day in the office, to tell everyone goodbye and express my deep appreciation to my work team. The Department of Works had a party for Mike and me. I remarked in my journal that saying the word "goodbye" is strange—it's so simple yet so significant. There should be more to it.

Auk nie, hold the countdown: Africa could always be counted on for a last-minute disorienting surprise.

During the countdown to our departure, Dorcas told us that when we returned from America, which to her we obviously would return, we were to bring money to buy a washing machine. Then she would use the washing machine to clean our clothes, and it would be much better for her. Dorcas asked if she could have our circular clothesline after we left our house. It was about five feet tall, a central metal pole with radial arms and a white cord strung between the arms in an octagon fashion. We said it would be our going-away present to her. It's hard to imagine for us, but a clothesline was a significant quality-of-life improvement for Dorcas, who hung her washing to dry on trees and bushes.

How the miscommunication occurred was never clear, but when Dorcas returned for her last workweek, she somehow got the misunderstanding that the clothesline would not be hers. Perhaps it was some muddled interpretation of our offer to take a new one to her later, so that we could leave the old one with the house.

Whatever the reason, Dorcas went into wailing hysterics, ululating in the shrill voice that Tswana women use at funerals. She collapsed in a fetal position in a corner of the kitchen, covering her head with her apron. She was inconsolable. No reassurances worked. Only pulling the clothesline out of the ground, bringing it into the kitchen, and physically offering it to her brought her out of the intense grief.

This was one of several incidents, like the lack of response to the fainting woman in Ann's bank, which are a mystery. Dealing with a cross-cultural problem, it's hard to know if there is a translation mistake, some obscure custom, or simply an eccentric personality. It's like working a jigsaw puzzle with all the pieces turned upside down.

In hindsight, Dorcas was from a people whose lives were filled with uncertainty due to capricious authorities. Perhaps for such a people, it was conceivable that her employers would break their pledge and jerk away a gift at the last moment.

Dorcas sent a letter to my mother, written by a friend or family member, which arrived in the US a few weeks after we had left. It is one of my most priceless treasures from Africa. A verbatim transcript:

> *P.O. Box*
> *Mafikeng*
> *8670*
> *27 September 1980*

Mrs Norton

> *I am stressing my sincerely Gratitude to Norton family when thinking about their Son BILL, who came here in South Africa with good Manners because charity begin at home.*

> *Mrs Norton, your son was very kind and polite to one another. He was very shy and I thought he is the youngest amongst the three i.e., from Joe, Mike. When he discovered I am angry to him instead of answering me, he can rather hide his face from me. May God bliss him and by the time he Marry a woman, may apply the same Manners to her without even a single word with his vocal cord.*
>
> *We stay together here in Africa Continent without any trouble and they clothed my children as their brother and sister. It didn't show that I was single to other African families.*
>
> *BILL NORTON May success be with you wherever you go, "Viva!!*
> *"BON VOYAGE AURI VORI [au revoir?]"*
>
> *Remember me to Norton family*
>
> *I remain*
> *DORCAS (Bill's Mother in Africa)*
>
> *Good Manners and Love to one another is what I discovered from all Americans.*

God bless you, Dorcas, my mother from Africa.

On September 29, my last day in Bophu, we cleaned out the house and performed last-minute errands in town. I sold my Risk game to Alex (I have always regretted not just giving it to him), which was something akin to Cortez burning his ships. Everything didn't fit in my bags, so at the last moment, I filled a box with odds and ends and Duane agreed to ship it home for me. (It arrived intact; thank you, Duane, and the Montshiwa post office.)

We made it to the Mafikeng railway station to catch our overnight train to Jo'burg with only fifteen minutes to spare. The Le Roux family all came to see me off and give me a going-away present. A smiling Steve Le Roux fussed at me in Afrikaans for being late, and then we all embraced.

My traveling companions and I boarded in a panic and suddenly, the train jerked and then groaned as if resisting our departure. The train slowly pulled away from the platform, and soon we were click-clacking into the twilight that was settling on the veld.

As I lay on my Pullman bed that evening swaying with the motion of the train, I could close my eyes and see faces: John and Lynn, the rest of the team, work friends, ministry friends, pastors and passengers, black faces, and white faces. I saw all their faces clearly in my mind's eye, but as the kilometers faded behind us, their faces got smaller and smaller and smaller ... until I drifted away in my last South African sleep.

At the Johannesburg airport, Amy and I had a last goodbye. It's tempting to compare our relationship to Rick and Ilsa's in *Casablanca*, when, after their brief romance and Rick's decision it could not continue, they parted on the airport tarmac in Africa to play their separate parts in the war. But this was not a movie with a grand ending. I flew on to the US to pursue my call as an engineer, and Amy continued to serve the Tswana in Montshiwa.

September 30 (In the air to Nairobi)

I don't know what for exactly, but I struggle to keep back tears. Is it her? Is it the team? It is the struggles of two years? I don't know.

Amy and I exchanged letters for some months after we parted in Johannesburg. Then, as expected, distance and time snuffed out the last spark like moist fingers on a candlewick. Two years after I returned to the US, I heard through mutual friends that Amy was engaged. By that time, so was I.

After our week in the Netherlands, Germany, and Switzerland, Mike and Steve had already left for flights home and it was down to Ann, Joe, his sister Mary, and me. We were going to split up in the Basel, Switzerland, train station. Ann and I were traveling different paths home than Joe and Mary. This was it.

A story in the Old Testament tells of two friends: Jonathan and David. Jonathan initiates a friendship with David, and Jonathan "loved David as himself." But there came a time when they had to separate, and both knew it could be forever. They wept together, but the Bible pointedly says, "But David wept the most." This is the story of Joe and me.

October 12 (On the train to Berlin)

It was a tearful parting between Ann and I and Joe in Basel. I've never had a friend like Joe who loved me and accepted me so unconditionally. He initiated our friendship but when we parted I was like David when he separated from Jonathan; I cried the most.

A Son of the South Returns

October 22 (In flight ~ 100 miles from Atlanta, the hills of North Georgia below)

SHEER JOY! Soon I'll be reunited with family and my country. Traveling since 7:30 pm (it's now 8:12 am) by bus, underground, train, and plane for this meeting. PTL that I'm here with all my belongings after travel halfway around the world. The plane is slowing, too excited to write!

At baggage claim, I found my huge California suitcase and my other luggage safe and sound. I had death-gripped my black-body Minolta on the plane, as I was wont to do after getting it back from "camera person." I breezed through passport control and customs. Then I could see my mom and my dad waving enthusiastically behind a glass wall across the concourse. I smiled and waved and started that way pushing a cart with my bags on it. I could see nothing else.

That is, until the two security officers stopped and questioned me. I assume a young man arriving alone with Amsterdam stamped in his passport was suspicious. In response to their questions about what I was bringing into the country, I showed them a small piece of South African *biltong*, jerky, I was carrying. The officers confiscated the biltong, but by freely offering it up, I apparently convinced them that I was not carrying any contraband and they let me go. It was funny—Africa reached out across the waves with a final surprise, a cellophane-wrapped gift of freedom.

Then I was across the floor and melted into the tears and hugs of my mom and my dad. My mom was wearing her unquenchable grin.

An African expression was quoted to us often during the last few days in Bophu: "Once you have tasted the waters of Africa, you will always be thirsty until you drink from them again."

As I write these last words, I find that, *auk*, I am so thirsty.

EPILOGUE

The eye never forgets what the heart has seen.
— African Proverb

My time in Bophu seems so short at the end of a four decade career. Yet it stands out like a still-glowing ember. The experience is like a rare treasure or, to borrow from scripture, like a pearl of great price.

After returning from Africa, I re-engaged with family and friends, entered the engineering workforce in Birmingham, and God led me to my lovely bride of forty years. The Bophu Department of Works sent a congratulatory telegram that my dad read at our wedding rehearsal. Three wonderful children came along with the intelligence and good looks of their mother. Our last child was a son; I named him after my teammate Joe.

It shouldn't be too surprising that we have a unique family attribute: wanderlust. Between the five of us, we have visited some forty countries for work, education, missions, and simply to see more of the world.

As I dreamed in Africa, I eventually earned an MBA degree and served in leadership and management roles for most of my career. I never managed an equipment fleet again, but as Mr. Masibi predicted, I learned a bit of human engineering in Bophu. These principles proved universal.

The spiritual ministry of my Bophu team, and the Crusade teams that followed, touched thousands and many discovered new lives of love, joy, and peace through faith in Jesus Christ. In our physical ministry through our government jobs, we made life better for many, many more. We had the honor of being a part of something extraordinary.

After the ANC was voted into power in the open election of 1994, apartheid was dismantled and all of the homelands, including Bophuthatswana, were re-united with South Africa. Sixteen years had elapsed from the inception of the Crusade ministry in Montshiwa. Who knows: as the children in Montshiwa grew up and entered adult society, perhaps the team's demonstration that black and white can live side by side eased the transition to a racially integrated society.

The Bophu team with spouses and children has gathered together for several reunions and there were always lots of kids. However, the children are grown now, and we fill their absence at our get-togethers by swapping grandkid pictures. Four of our number earned doctorates, and six of the original fourteen served in occupational ministry their entire careers. John's wife, Lynn, was called to heaven early and we all miss her. And yes, the team romance mentioned in the story had a fairy-tale ending: Duane and Bonnie fell in love in Africa and were married soon after they returned to the States.

Whenever we are together, we reminisce as if it all happened last week instead of forty years ago. The stories seem to get funnier, or more poignant, as the years go by. I stand back and marvel at our lasting comradery. How much richer my life has been for filling in that Crusade preference form with, "I want to be placed *anywhere* ..."

NOTES

Chapter 1
1. The timing of the layers of shock amplified the traumatic stress. A common reaction to such stress is to rebel against the prior life to gain control of the future. However, the precipitating events do not change responsibility; the choices were mine. Counseling might have helped but was not a consideration. At the time, seeking mental healthcare, if it had even been available, was seen as a weakness (among other misconceptions). If the reader or a loved one has experienced an extremely stressful event(s) at a young age, he or she is encouraged to connect with a mental health professional who has expertise in life's stressors and who follows Jesus Christ.
2. Jerome Lawrence and Robert E. Lee, *Inherit the Wind*, paperback ed. (New York: Ballantine Books, an imprint of The Random House Publishing Group, 2003), 93.

Chapter 2
1. 1. John Piper, *What Jesus Demands from the World*, paperback ed. (Wheaton, IL: Crossway, 2006; Trade Paperback, 2011), 373-74. Citation refers to the paperback edition.

Chapter 3
1. Probably a congenital cardiac shunt: a communication between heart chambers that causes an abnormal blood flow within the heart.

Chapter 14
1. C. S. Lewis, *The Problem of Pain*, paperback ed. (New York: HarperCollins Publishers, 2001), 88-89.
2. C. S. Lewis, *The Four Loves*, paperback ed. (New York: HarperOne, an imprint of HarperCollins Publishers, 2017), 114.
3. Bill Ewing with Donna Wallace and Todd Hillard, *Rest Assured* (Rapid City, SD: Real Life Press, 2003), 111.

Chapter 15
1. Eugene Marais, "Winternag," from *Afrikaans Poems with English Translations* compiled by Hennie van Coller, Helize van Vuuren,

and Louise Viljoen (Pretoria: Protea Boekhuis, 2018), 12. Used with permission.

Chapter 16
1. Frank Welsh, *A History of South Africa*, paperback ed. (London: HarperCollins Publishers, 2000), 489.
2. Welsh, 489.
3. Ernest Cole, *House of Bondage* (New York: Random House, 1967), 52.
4. Jeffrey Butler, Robert I. Rotberg, and John Adams, *The Black Homelands of South Africa*, paperback ed. (Berkeley and Los Angeles: University of California Press, 1978), 4. Derived from population data.
5. Welsh, 488.
6. *All the Facts about South Africa* (Washington, D.C.: South African Embassy, The Information Counsellor, February 1978), 10.
7. Welsh, 477.
8. Welsh, 474-475.
9. Nik Ripken, *The Insanity of God* (Nashville: B&H Publishing Group, 2013), 76.

Chapter 17
1. Vic Mayhew, ed., *Illustrated Guide to Southern Africa* (Cape Town: The Reader's Digest Association South Africa, 1978), 273.
2. John Eldredge, *The Journey of Desire*, paperback ed. (Nashville: Nelson Books, 2016), 202.
3. John Eldredge, *Wild at Heart* (Nashville: Thomas Nelson, 2001), 30.
4. C. S. Lewis, *The Lion, the Witch, and the Wardrobe*, paperback ed. (New York: Macmillan Publishing Co., First Collier book edition, 1970), 75-76.

Chapter 19
1. C. S. Lewis, *The Voyage of the Dawn Treader*, paperback ed. (New York: Macmillan Publishing Co., First Collier book edition, 1970), 90.

Chapter 20
1. Eldredge, *The Journey of Desire*, 48-49.
2. Cole, 150.

Chapter 22
1. Butler, 14.

Chapter 23
1. Matthew Henry, *Matthews Henry's Concise Commentary on the Whole Bible* (Nashville: Thomas Nelson, Inc., 1997), 880.
2. William Barclay, *The Gospel of Matthew Volume 2* (Edinburgh: The Saint Andrew Press, 1958; Philadelphia: The Westminster Press), 19.
3. David Guzik, "Is 'Normal Life' a Calling from God?" *Enduring Word Q&A,* online video recorded February 21, 2020, 9:37, https://enduringword.com/category/q-a-with-pastor-david/page/12/.
4. Amanda Jenkins, Kristen Hendricks, and Dallas Jenkins, *The Chosen: Forty Days with Jesus* (Savage, MN: BroadStreet Publishing Group, LLC., 2019), 160.

Chapter 24
1. Welsh, 458.
2. Lewis, *The Four Loves,* 167.
3. *A Guide to Reentry*, January 1980 Field Test Copy, Campus Crusade for Christ, 3.

PHOTOS

Chapter 1. Mafeking airstrip terminal. The name of the town was changed to Mafikeng when it was incorporated into Bophuthatswana on September 1, 1980.

Chapter 2. Agape Movement promotional literature.

Chapter 3. South Africa's escarpment near Blyde River Canyon (now Motlase Canyon).

Chapter 4. Hotel Antonieta, Tijuana. AIT students had two cross-cultural stints in Mexico.

Chapter 5. The team (less one). The author is on the back row far right.

Chapter 6. Montshiwa house #2293 and the VW kombi.

Chapter 7. Two Montshiwa children. In the background are the older "matchbox" township houses.

Chapter 8. Teammates and the author with a Department of Works official wearing a safari suit.

Chapter 9. The team singles and the kombi, probably in downtown Durban.

Chapter 10. Bophu singles in Royal Natal National Park.

Chapter 11. Letters to/from home.

Chapter 12. Man in hat: friend of the ministry; paper boy on the streets of Mafikeng; donkey cart from an outlying village; construction for the new Mmabatho and a typical Tswana lady carrying her shopping balanced on her head (no hands required).

Chapter 13. Pictorial evangelistic tract for nonreaders.

Chapter 14. Workshop mechanics and earth mover at a Department of Works reservoir project.

Chapter 15. View of the veld and acacia thorn trees.

Chapter 16. Soccer with neighborhood boys.

Chapter 17. Cheetah couple posing in Kruger National Park.

Chapter 18. Office in the antiquated Imperial Reserve, Department of Works headquarters.

Chapter 19. Hills and fields of Swaziland (now Eswatini).

Chapter 20. New Department of Works motor grader (YB tag above windshield).

Chapter 21. Here's Life campaign banners.

Chapter 22. Here's Life seminar.

Chapter 23. The bushveld, wooded area of the veld.

Chapter 24. Bophu soldier on guard during the transfer of Mafikeng to Bophuthatswana.

Chapter 25. Dust storm sweeping through Montshiwa.

Chapter 26. Roommates taking tea on the back stoop of house #2293.

Epilogue.　Tswana chief or headman's home.

ABOUT THE AUTHOR

After returning from South Africa, Bill's ministry was redirected to work, church, and family. His career evolved into management roles in engineering and marketing. While working, Bill earned a master's degree in engineering from the University of Alabama at Birmingham and an MBA from Vanderbilt University where he received the Leadership in Executive Education Award. Bill is a registered Professional Engineer.

Bill and his wife, Lori, and their grown children have made international connections a family tradition. One or more have stood on six continents (still working toward Antarctica). The entire family are also loyal alumni of Auburn University. The family sponsors an Auburn scholarship to encourage students to study abroad.

Currently, Bill writes for periodicals, engages in business consulting, and volunteers with civic and charitable organizations. Bill and Lori are members of The Church at Brook Hills in Birmingham. They enjoy entertaining their grandchildren at the family's "farmette" in the Dunnavant Valley, Alabama.

CPSIA information can be obtained
at www.ICGtesting.com
Printed in the USA
JSHW071722040323
38329JS00005B/57